❧ BEST-EVER ❧
CHOCOLATE DESSERTS

RICK RODGERS

CONTEMPORARY
BOOKS

CHICAGO

Library of Congress Cataloging-in-Publication Data

Rodgers, Rick, 1953–
    Best-ever chocolate desserts / Rick Rodgers.
        p.   cm.
    Includes index
    ISBN 0-8092-4028-9 (pbk.)
    1. Chocolate.   2. Desserts.   I. Title.
TX767.C5R63   1992
641.6'374—dc20   91-35619
                                          CIP

Published by Contemporary Books, Inc.
180 North Michigan Avenue, Chicago, Illinois 60601
Manufactured in the United States of America
International Standard Book Number: 0-8092-4028-9

To Mom and Dad: Because of your example,
I know the importance of filling one's life
with good friends and good food.

Contents

Preface   vii

Acknowledgments   xi

1   Getting to Know Chocolate   1

2   Basic Chocolate Techniques   7

3   Other Ingredients   9

4   The Finishing Touch   13

5   From Grandma's Cake Stand   15

6   Star-Spangled Sweets   41

7   A Taste of Europe   77

8   Bow-Tie Desserts   111

9   At the Soda Fountain   137

Index   159

Preface

❧

It's luxurious yet affordable. Sensuous but innocent enough for a child to enjoy. It can be homey and wholesome or sophisticated and decadent. It's . . . chocolate!

America has had a long love affair with chocolate. (America's first chocolate factory was established in Boston in 1765 by Dr. James Baker, and Baker's Chocolate thrives today.) Over the last decade chocolate consumption has increased from 8½ to more than 11 pounds per capita. Chocolate manufacturing influences many other commodities. More than 3½ million quarts of whole milk are used *daily* in U.S. chocolate production.

Chocolate is an undeniably important part of our culinary heritage. (It is interesting to note that while today's chocolate is a dessert that the whole family shares, it was imported to the Spanish court from Mexico not as a sweet but as a celebrated aphrodisiac!) Most Americans grew up with a favorite chocolate cake, chocolate chip cookie, brownie, or candy bar. Re-creating these wonderful recipes satisfies both our physical and emotional needs. *Best-Ever Chocolate Desserts* is jam-packed with these memorable recipes and more.

I am often asked how I became a professional chocolate aficionado. (I am actively campaigning to abolish the negative-sounding word *chocoholic*.) For many years I was a caterer in Manhattan, and chocolate desserts always made a spectacular finale to an elegant sit-down meal. I thought of serving bite-size chocolate truffles at the end of a cocktail party as well. Often members of the press would attend these parties. One night a lovely blonde lady came into the kitchen, raving about my truffles. Her name was Joan Steuer, and she was the editor of a magazine dedicated strictly to the pleasures of chocolate, *Chocolatier*. At Joan's invitation I began writing articles for *Chocolatier*, sharing my years of baking experience with its readers. Soon I was working steadily at the magazine as test kitchen associate, at the side of one of the great chocolatiers, Adrienne

Welch. It became obvious that chocolate and I were "meant for each other," and I began studying "the food of the gods" in earnest, with learning trips to confectionery schools and bakeries in Paris, Vienna, New York, and Zurich.

In *Best-Ever Chocolate Desserts*, I offer the best recipes from my collection. A great recipe doesn't have to be expensive or hard to make. I crave a chewy chocolate chip cookie more often than fancy Baked Alaska. But there are chocolate chip cookies and *chocolate chip cookies*. As a cooking school teacher, a judge at many a chocolate cooking contest, a food writer for a dessert magazine, and a caterer, I've enjoyed enough chocolate delicacies to establish pretty strong criteria for "best-ever" desserts. The following array of sweets reflects that point of view.

In "From Grandma's Cake Stand," I've gathered all those delectable old-fashioned cakes from our culinary past. Here's where to find the Ultimate Devil's Food Cake with Fudgy Frosting, a moist and nutty Banana-Chocolate Loaf Cake, and my favorite layer cake—Black and White Layer Cake, fudgy layers with a fluffy white frosting.

I never could fathom the saying "As American as apple pie." Certainly apple pie was around for centuries in Europe before we started baking it over here! Now, chocolate chip cookies . . . that's another thing. "As American as a chocolate chip cookie" has such a nice ring, don't you think? In "Star-Spangled Desserts," you'll find a whole assortment of those All-American goodies we often found tucked into our lunch boxes or wished that we had. They include a large variety of drop and bar cookies, including brownies, blondies, and "born in the U.S.A." candies like fudge (two versions) and rocky road.

"A Taste of Europe" features recipes collected on my many trips over the years. Some of them (such as Sachertorte) are right off the marble-topped dessert tables of famous Viennese coffeehouses. The complex but exquisite Marjolaine Classique is a star of French *pâtisserie* and is joined by other members in that fabulous firmament. I learned a lot about chocolate (and self-control in the face of food) in Switzerland and brought back a recipe for one of my favorites, Swiss Truffle Loaf. Italy is represented here by a chocolate and cheese Tiramisù and Spuma di Caffé Latte, a mocha-flavored mousse.

As a former actor I can't resist that element of "drama" in special celebratory meals. I orchestrate a fine dinner like an exciting night at the theater. First, an overture (hors d'oeuvre) to precede a stirring first act (the first course). Of course the second act must have some "meat" to it (the entrée), and the awe-inspiring finale (dessert) should leave you wanting more. In "Bow-Tie Desserts," I'll divulge the extraspecial desserts that put my catering business on the map. Some of these recipes may take a little bit of work, but the results are well worth the effort. A Bittersweet Lemon Tart is the perfect way to end an elegant supper. Or, for the special person in your life, make the White Chocolate Celebration Cake, decorated with bunches of sugar-glazed roses.

When I was 15 years old, my first job was in a neighborhood ice-cream fountain. It turned out to be the beginning of a minicareer as a soda jerk. I reached the pinnacle of my "profession" in college, when I worked at San Francisco's ultimate ice-cream emporium, Blum's. "At the Soda Fountain" will share the secrets of the trade so you can create those frozen fantasies at home. This is the realm of chewy, gooey hot fudge sauces, thick chocolate malteds, and sky-high sundaes. The chapter also includes my versions of baked goods that are often offered at soda fountains and luncheonettes, such as Parker House Cream Pie.

Anyone who has picked up this book already joins me in saying "I never met a chocolate dessert I didn't like." However, after trying a few of the recipes from this sumptuous assortment, you'll agree that these are truly chocolate's best-ever desserts.

Acknowledgments

I first met Diane Kniss when our catering companies combined to create a chocolate buffet for a mutual client. Since then, she has given me immeasurable amounts of time and expertise, and I am grateful, as always, that chocolate brought us together. Lisa Van Riper of Baker's Chocolate and Mary Solomon of Hershey's Food Corporation arranged for generous amounts of their excellent products to be delivered to my kitchen. And thank you to three ladies who are always there when good times are to be had and chocolate is to be savored—Mary Goodbody, Joan Steuer, and Adrienne Welch. But thanks especially to Patrick Fisher, who has never once said, "What? Chocolate AGAIN?!!"

1
Getting to Know Chocolate

Chocolate is one of the kitchen's most temperamental ingredients. It is composed of more than 96 different highly volatile enzymes, and they are all fighting for attention. If you learn to understand chocolate's eccentricities, sweet success can be yours.

How Chocolate Is Made

Chocolate making is a complicated procedure. Cacao trees are grown only in the tropics of Latin America and West Africa, and each tree variety yields beans with different characteristics that can be blended, not unlike varying grapes going into wine. The multicolored cacao pods are collected from the trees, fermented briefly to age the beans inside, sun-dried for a week, then shipped to the manufacturer's roasting plant. That plant can be in Zurich, Switzerland, or Hershey, Pennsylvania, among other locations. The pods are roasted carefully (like coffee). The length of the roast is an important factor in the flavor of the finished chocolate. For example, some chocolates will have a signature "high roast" note that is almost espressolike.

The pods are next hulled to harvest the beans. (Cacao pods are sold in nurseries as mulch.) The beans are ground, or "conched," and again, this is a critical procedure. A long conching period gives the smoothest-melting chocolate. European chocolates are generally conched longest (48–72 hours), and this translates into a more expensive product.

After the cacao beans are conched, they form a pasty mass called *chocolate liquor*. Chocolate liquor is the basic ingredient in chocolate manufacturing, and each manufacturer sweetens and flavors it to a specific formulation. Or the chocolate liquor can be pressed hydraulically, which will extract most of the ivory-colored cocoa butter. The cocoa butter can be processed separately into cosmetic products or used later in the chocolate-making procedure. The chocolate mass that has most of the cocoa butter removed is dried and ground into cocoa powder.

Types of Chocolate

Each brand of chocolate is made from the manufacturer's own proprietary formula. It is important to know what brands of chocolate were used in recipe testing, because varying brands will give fluctuations in texture, baking times, appearance, and flavor. (I'm not saying that if you deviate from my chosen brands the recipes won't work, but they will be different.) However, the Food and Drug Administration (FDA) has set Standards of Identification for the various types of chocolate. These Standards state the different ingredients that must be present in chocolate and cocoa products and the range of percentages for each. For example, semisweet chocolate can contain anywhere from 15 to 35 percent chocolate liquor.

Unsweetened Chocolate

Unsweetened chocolate is chocolate liquor that has been cooled and molded into blocks. It is also known as *baking* or *bitter chocolate*. Unsweetened chocolate is not very tasty on its own and is always combined with other, more palatable ingredients. I used Baker's unsweetened chocolate when testing recipes in this book.

Bittersweet Chocolate

It can be argued that bittersweet and semisweet chocolates can be used interchangeably. The FDA standards allow for so many variances in the amounts of ingredients used that one company's bittersweet can be another's semisweet. Therefore, it's difficult to unequivocally state that bittersweet is always less sweet than semisweet, but that is a good rule of thumb. Generally, if the recipe is European in origin or character, I use bittersweet chocolate. I identify bittersweet chocolate as being in the European style, which is smooth-melting with a high percentage of cocoa butter. I use Lindt Excellence bittersweet chocolate.

Many specialty grocers carry couverture chocolate, which is generally used for chocolate molding. When doing chocolate molding or dipping, couverture chocolate needs to be tempered, a complicated professional procedure that stabilizes the chocolate so that it retains its shape at room temperature after unmolding. As none of the recipes in this book require tempered chocolate, I am not going to give directions for the procedure. It is important to know that couverture chocolate has a very high percentage of added cocoa butter (ensuring a high gloss, a thin coat, and a crisp snap when you bite into the product). This extra fat must be compensated for in the recipe, so reduce any butter by 1 tablespoon for every 8 ounces of couverture.

Semisweet Chocolate

To me semisweet chocolate is an American-style chocolate with lots of chocolate impact. I use pound after pound of it in my kitchen, particularly in old-fashioned desserts like frosted layer cakes. Baker's semisweet chocolate was used in these recipes.

Sweet Chocolate

Sweet chocolate is a variation of semisweet chocolate with a higher sugar content. Baker's German's Sweet Chocolate is the most widely available, and that is what I used. If you must substitute sweet chocolate for semisweet, reduce the sugar in your recipe by 1 tablespoon for every ounce of sweet chocolate.

Milk Chocolate

While milk chocolate is America's favorite eating chocolate, it is hard to use in baking. Milk chocolate contains dried milk powder and a high proportion of sugar, so it doesn't blend well with other ingredients in a batter. However, there is more than one way to get the goodness of milk chocolate into your recipe, as illustrated in Peanut Butter and Milk Chocolate Brownies. I used Hershey's milk chocolate.

White Chocolate

White chocolate is created from cocoa butter flavored with dried milk solids, sugar, and vanilla. Because it does not contain any chocolate liquor, the FDA does not consider it "real chocolate," so you will find it labeled under such confusing names as "Swiss Confectionery Bar." Always read the label to be sure your white chocolate is made from cocoa butter and not inexpensive substitutes such as vegetable shortenings or coconut oils. Good white chocolate has an ivory, not paper-white, color. I use Lindt Blancor. White chocolate can be difficult to melt, becoming grainy in texture if mishandled. Be careful of melting white chocolate on humid days, when moisture in the air seems to make the milk proteins in the chocolate swell. These pesky milk proteins also scorch easily, so melt the white chocolate carefully. (See "Melting Chocolate" in Chapter 2.)

Unsweetened Cocoa Powder

Cocoa powder is chocolate liquor with about 25 percent of the cocoa butter removed. The amount of cocoa butter varies from brand to brand, but this is of no concern to most consumers, unless you are making cocoa-based diet recipes. It is, however, very important to know the difference between nonalkalized and alkalized cocoa powders, since the packages rarely indicate the variety on the label.

Nonalkalized (natural) cocoa powder is familiar as Hershey's Cocoa in the brown box. (I used Hershey's Cocoa in these recipes.) Natural cocoa has a rich, full chocolate flavor. Cocoa is a highly acidic product, as are buttermilk, brown sugar, and some other baking ingredients. When the acidic cocoa is mixed with an alkali (such as baking soda) and moistened, the two react to create carbon dioxide. This gas is trapped in the batter and makes your baked goods rise.

Alkalized or Dutch-process cocoa powder has been treated with an alkali solution to remove some of the cocoa's acidity, which gives it a darker color and mellower flavor. (The alkalizing procedure was developed in the Netherlands, hence the term "Dutch-process.") However, with the acidity reduced, Dutch-process cocoa will not react properly with baking soda. A cake made with these ingredients may not rise properly and might have a soapy taste. Use this rule of thumb: if the cake recipe calls for baking soda, use a nonalkalized cocoa like Hershey's (in the brown box). If it calls for baking powder (which combines dry acid and alkali components so you are not dependent on the acids found in your batter's ingredients), you can use either nonalkalized or Dutch-process cocoa. When I want a Dutch-process cocoa, I use Hershey's European-Style Cocoa (in the silver box) or Droste.

Compound Coatings and Premelted Chocolates

I avoid chocolate compound coatings (also called summer coatings), which replace cocoa butter with vegetable shortening as their base and use plenty of artificial flavorings. Compound coatings are normally displayed right next to the real chocolate, so beware. I also shun the premelted chocolate, which is simply unsweetened chocolate mixed with enough vegetable oil to keep it in a liquid state—I don't need extra oils in my baked goods, thank you.

Chocolate Chips

Chocolate chips are morsels of chocolate that have an extra measure of lecithin, a natural emulsifier found in most chocolate products that helps them keep their shape in the oven. Chocolate chips normally have a stronger, harsher flavor than regular chocolate, since they must retain their character when buried inside a cookie, cake, or other product. While you certainly can substitute chips for

4

chopped chocolate, ounce for ounce the chips are more difficult to melt due to the lecithin, and the flavor will not be as refined. I used Baker's semisweet chocolate chips most often. For variety, I will use Hershey's milk chocolate chips and Reese's peanut butter chips, although they cannot be melted and substituted for regular chocolate in recipes.

Cocoa Butter

The cocoa butter naturally found in chocolate is the "secret ingredient" that makes it so wonderful. Cocoa butter (and therefore chocolate) is one of the very few foods that melts at a temperature below our body's 98.6°F. That is why chocolate melts immediately in your mouth, creating such a marvelous sensation. You will rarely cook with cocoa butter on its own, but I mention it here to caution you to read chocolate products' labels. They should include cocoa butter, not cheaper fats like vegetable shortening. And remember that any product that is labeled "chocolate-flavored" doesn't have enough chocolate liquor in it to be called true chocolate and is normally bolstered with artificial flavorings. Some "chocolate" chips, for example, are really "chocolate-flavored," so beware. You will compromise the flavor of a dessert with these less expensive products.

2
Basic Chocolate Techniques

Chopping Chocolate

Chopping chocolate properly will ensure smooth and speedy melting. As a rule of thumb, remember that the greater the surface area, the more uniform the melt. Therefore, finely chopped chocolate spread over the bottom of a double boiler will melt more quickly and evenly than large pieces. I define *finely chopped chocolate* as pieces less than ¼ inch square. *Coarsely chopped chocolate* is chopped into pieces about ½ inch square and is generally used as chunks in a batter.

A large sharp chef's knife is best for chopping chocolate. Use a dry, odor-free cutting surface, preferably plastic. If you do a lot of baking at home, you should really have two separate chopping boards—one for sweet ingredients (chocolate, nuts, dried fruits) and one for savory (garlic, onions, and herbs). This will prevent garlic-flavored brownies. Do not chop chocolate in a food processor, as it may melt from the resulting friction.

Melting Chocolate

Knowing how to melt chocolate properly is a valuable skill to have, since most recipes call for this step. I use only two pieces of equipment for melting—double boiler or a microwave oven. In either procedure chocolate is very susceptible to heat and moisture so remember these guidelines:

Beware of overheating chocolate. Whenever chocolate is exposed to temperatures above 125°F, it may scorch, lose flavor, and "seize," or tighten and become grainy.

Chocolate hates moisture, so never let any liquid get into melting chocolate (unless called for in a recipe), or it will "bind," or thicken. Melt chocolate uncovered; condensation that would collect on the lid could drip down into the double boiler insert. While a single drop of moisture can ruin a batch of melted chocolate, chocolate will melt without binding in larger amounts of liquid—about 2 tablespoons of liquid to each ounce of chocolate.

Chocolate that binds or seizes can sometimes be rescued. Try stirring in about 1 teaspoon of solid vegetable shortening (not butter or margarine, which includes water) for every 2 ounces of melted chocolate, stirring until smooth.

Double Boiler Method

Heat the finely chopped chocolate in the top part of an uncovered double boiler over very hot, but not simmering, water, stirring occasionally until it is melted and smooth. The double boiler insert should be above, not in, the water. Milk and white chocolates: have high proportions of milk proteins, butter fats, and sugar that clump and burn easily and are melted most successfully if hot tap water (not over 125°F) touches the bottom of the insert. Another tip for delicate milk and white chocolates: heat half of the chocolate first, stirring occasionally until it is almost melted. Then add the remaining chocolate to the melted batch, which will act as a buffer, and continue melting.

Microwave Method

Place the finely chopped chocolate in a microwave-proof bowl and microwave at 50 percent power for 2–4 minutes, interrupting the procedure every 30 seconds to stir. The chocolate may not always appear melted and must be stirred for at least 30 seconds until smooth. I call for the double boiler method of melting since not everyone owns a microwave. But I admit that I always melt my chocolate in the microwave.

Storing Chocolate

If chocolate is exposed to high temperatures during storage, the cocoa butter will separate from the solids, collecting and hardening on the surface. This unattractive streaking is called *bloom*. Bloomed chocolate is harmless enough in recipes where the chocolate is to be melted and baked in a batter, but it is visually unappealing in its unmelted state.

To store chocolate properly, wrap it in aluminum foil and then plastic wrap to provide a barrier to moisture, light, and foreign odors. Store it in a cool, dry place with good ventilation and out of sunlight. (My kitchen is very sunny, and having 10 pounds of chocolate melt accidentally on one hot summer day, I now store my chocolate in a cool closet.) Ideal storage temperature is 60–75°F, which means the humid refrigerator is out!

3
Other Ingredients

Butter

Unsalted butter, also called *sweet butter*, is used in all recipes. Salt was added to butter starting in the early 20th century to hide any off flavors and to prolong the shelf life of the product. I believe unsalted butter has a fresher, more natural flavor. If you are using salted butter, decrease any salt in the recipe to taste. I *never* use margarine, as I find its taste unpleasant. But *you* may use margarine instead of butter if you wish.

To soften cold butter quickly for creaming purposes, grate the butter coarsely into the mixing bowl, then proceed with the recipe. Or use my favorite method: Unwrap the butter, cut it into pieces, then microwave at LOW (10 percent) power. Allow about 1 minute for a 4-ounce stick (8 tablespoons) to soften. The butter should be barely softened and pliable, not shiny and greasy.

Eggs

USDA grade A large eggs are used in all recipes. Always store your eggs in the refrigerator. If a recipe calls for whole eggs at room temperature, you may quickly bring the eggs to the proper temperature by placing chilled, unbroken eggs in a bowl filled with hot tap water and letting them stand for 5 minutes. Chilled eggs separate more easily, but egg whites beat to their fullest capacity if at room temperature. To bring chilled whites to the proper temperature, place them in a heatproof bowl set in a larger bowl of hot tap water. After washing your hands well, stir the eggs with your finger until they feel lukewarm. Remove the bowl from the water and beat.

Flour

Unbleached all-purpose, bleached all-purpose, and cake flours are not interchangeable. They all have varying amounts of gluten, the protein that makes batters and doughs hold together. The higher the flour's protein content, the tougher the finished product will be.

Unbleached flour is about 14 percent protein, making it best for yeast doughs and breads. All-purpose bleached flour (with a medium strength protein percentage of about 10 percent) was developed to be used in a variety of baked goods but is best in pies, cookies, and cakes. Cake flour (about 6 percent protein) makes the tenderest cakes. None of these recipes uses self-rising flour, which has leavenings already added. Be sure to use the flour that is specified in the recipe.

I measure my flour by the dip-and-scoop method: dip the measuring cup into the bag or container of flour and level off the top with a knife. Use proper measuring cups for your ingredients: metal measuring cups for dry ingredients and glass measuring cups with pouring spouts for liquids.

Nuts

Toasting nuts before stirring them into batters enhances the flavor of both the nuts and the dessert. To toast almonds, pecans, walnuts, and hazelnuts, place the nuts in a single layer on a baking sheet. Bake them in a preheated 350°F oven for 8-10 minutes, shaking the pan a couple of times, until the nuts are lightly browned and fragrant. (Macadamia nuts take slightly less time.) Let the nuts cool completely before chopping them.

To skin hazelnuts, wrap the warm toasted hazelnuts in a clean kitchen towel and let them stand for about 10 minutes. Using the towel, rub off as much of the skins as possible. (You can never get all of the skins off, so don't try. A little hazelnut skin never hurt anyone.)

Some recipes call for unsalted cashews, peanuts, or macadamia nuts, which are more commonly found in salted versions (although they are often available unsalted in health food stores). To remove salt, place the nuts in a wire sieve and rinse thoroughly under cold running water. Drain them well and pat dry with paper towels.

Sugar

Granulated sugar is used in most recipes, measured by the dip-and-scoop method. Although dark brown sugar has slightly more molasses in it, light and dark sugars can generally be interchanged with little difference in taste or appearance in the final dessert. Some recipes call for superfine sugar, also labeled *instant dissolving* sugar. If you can't find it in your market, simply whirl an equal amount of granulated sugar in a blender or food processor for a minute or two until it is finely ground.

Dairy Products

I prefer pasteurized heavy (or "whipping") cream to the "ultra-pasteurized" variety because the pasteurized version has a more natural taste and whips up thicker. Ultra-pasteurized cream has been cooked to such a high temperature that the flavor is affected. It tastes like evaporated milk to me. While it can be hard to locate a source (check dairy stores), once you taste the pasteurized cream, I'm sure you'll prefer it, too.

Many of the recipes in this book call for buttermilk. You can substitute regular milk for buttermilk if you sour it first. Stir about 1½ teaspoons fresh lemon juice or white vinegar to each ½ cup of regular milk. Let the mixture stand at room temperature for about 10 minutes, until curdled, then proceed with the recipe.

4
The Finishing Touch

Here are some ideas for easy, elegant ways to add a special fillip to your finished chocolate creations.

Chocolate Curls

Use a large chunk of any flavor chocolate, such as "break-up" chocolate, premium bulk chocolate (available at candy stores or specialty grocers), or a 1-ounce square of packaged supermarket chocolate.

1. The chocolate must be at the proper temperature: warm room temperature with low humidity. If the chocolate is too cold, it will splinter and not curl. If your first attempts cause splintering, warm the chocolate by using either of these techniques:

   a. Place the chocolate directly under a table lamp, about 12 inches from the bulb. (A reading lamp with a flexible neck works well.) Let stand until the surface of the chocolate is warm but not melting, about 5 minutes.

   b. Warm the chocolate in a microwave oven set at MEDIUM (50 percent) power for 30 seconds. I usually use the microwave method.

2. Use a paper towel to hold the chocolate in one hand so the heat from your fingers doesn't melt the chocolate. Using a swivel-bladed vegetable peeler, make the chocolate curls by pressing down while you "peel" from the upper edge of the smooth side of the chocolate chunk toward you. The harder you press, the thicker the curls. Let the curls fall onto a wax paper–lined baking sheet, then refrigerate until ready to use.

   If the chocolate is too warm, it will form soft strips that you still may be able to curl with your fingers.

Chocolate Leaves

Use firm, clean, nontoxic leaves such as lemon, ivy, galax, or camellia leaves. Rinse the leaves, then pat them completely dry.

1. In the top part of a double boiler over hot, not simmering, water, melt 2–4 ounces of chocolate, stirring occasionally, until smooth. (See "Melting Chocolate" in Chapter 2 for specific instructions.) Let the chocolate cool for about 10 minutes, until tepid and slightly thickened.

2. Hold a leaf in the palm of your hand and, using the back of a teaspoon, coat the underside of the leaf evenly and thinly with the melted chocolate. Avoid getting the chocolate on the other side of the leaf, or it may break while peeling.

3. Refrigerate the coated leaves on a wax paper–lined baking sheet until the chocolate is firm. Carefully peel the leaves away from the chocolate and then refrigerate the chocolate leaves until ready to use.

Other Decorating Tips

These garnishes look great arranged in a circle around the top of a frosted cake:

- Hazelnuts, walnuts, pecans, or almonds, half dipped in chocolate
- Fresh strawberries, dried thoroughly, half dipped in chocolate. Or use dried apricot halves or dried pineapple chunks.
- Chocolate-dipped espresso beans
- Grand Marnier Truffles (see Index)

5
From Grandma's Cake Stand

Double Chocolate–Sour Cream Layer Cake
The Original German Chocolate Cake with Coconut-Pecan Frosting
Chocolate Mayonnaise Cake with Easy Cocoa Frosting
Chocolate Pound Cake
Black and White Layer Cake
Cocoa Angel Food Cake with Strawberry Whip
Chocolate Zucchini Cake
Chocolate-Buttermilk Snackin' Cake
The Ultimate Devil's Food Cake with Fudgy Frosting
Wicky Wacky Chocolate Cake
Orange-Chocolate Bundt Cake
Banana-Chocolate Loaf Cake

Double Chocolate–Sour Cream Layer Cake

For fans of tart and sweet flavor combinations, here's a chocolate layer cake that makes the most of that delightful duo. Both cake and frosting are as easy as, well, pie. They both feature chocolate and sour cream, and they are both one-bowl recipes that can be whipped up in a flash.

CAKE
8 tablespoons (1 stick) unsalted butter, cut into pieces and softened
3 ounces unsweetened chocolate, chopped fine
1 cup boiling water
2 cups packed light brown sugar
2¼ cups cake flour
1½ teaspoons baking soda
½ teaspoon salt
2 large eggs, at room temperature
½ cup sour cream, at room temperature
1 teaspoon vanilla extract

FROSTING
12 ounces semisweet chocolate, chopped fine
1 cup sour cream, chilled
1 teaspoon vanilla extract
⅛ teaspoon salt

1. *Make the cake:* Position a rack in the center of the oven and preheat to 350°F. Lightly butter the insides of two 8-inch round baking pans. Line the bottoms of the pans with rounds of wax paper. Dust the sides of the pans with flour, tapping out any excess.

2. In a large bowl, melt the butter and chocolate in the boiling water and whisk until smooth. Using a hand-held electric mixer set at medium speed, beat in the brown sugar, cake flour, baking soda, and salt. Add the eggs, sour cream, and vanilla. Increase the speed to high and beat, scraping down the sides of the bowl as necessary with a rubber spatula, for 1 minute, until well blended. Transfer the batter to the prepared pans, smoothing the tops with the spatula.

3. Bake until a toothpick inserted in the center of the cakes comes out clean, 25–30 minutes. Cool on wire cake racks for 10 minutes. Run a sharp knife around the edges of the cakes to loosen them from the sides of the pans. Invert the cakes onto the wire cake racks. Carefully peel off the wax paper. Turn the cakes right side up and cool completely.

4. *Make the frosting:* In the top part of a double boiler set over hot, not simmering, water, melt the chocolate, stirring often, until smooth. Transfer the melted chocolate to a medium bowl. Add the sour cream, vanilla, and salt and whisk just until the mixture forms soft peaks.

5. *Assemble the cake:* Place one cake layer upside down on a serving platter. Spread the layer with about ½ cup of the frosting, then top with the other layer, right side up. Frost the top and sides of the cake with the remaining frosting. (The cake can be prepared up to 1 day ahead, covered with plastic wrap, and stored at room temperature.)

Makes 8–10 servings

Chocolate Morsels: If the frosting seems too soft to spread, place the bowl in a larger bowl of iced water. Let the frosting stand, whisking occasionally, until cool enough to beat to the desired consistency.

The Original German Chocolate Cake with Coconut-Pecan Frosting

German chocolate cake (named not after the country but after a Mr. German who worked for Baker's Chocolate and perfected the recipe for the sweet cooking chocolate that bears his name) is such a permanent fixture on the American dessert table that I assumed it was aeons old. Actually, I discovered it became popular only in the late fifties, based on a recipe from a Texas home cook. There are many versions of this exceptional layer cake, but this is the best, with lots of that scrumptious frosting.

CAKE
1 4-ounce package German's
   Sweet Chocolate, chopped fine
½ cup boiling water
2 cups all-purpose flour
1 teaspoon baking soda
½ teaspoon salt
1 cup (2 sticks) unsalted butter,
   softened
2 cups granulated sugar
4 large eggs, separated, at room
   temperature
1 teaspoon vanilla extract
1 cup buttermilk

FROSTING
1 12-ounce can evaporated milk
1½ cups granulated sugar
12 tablespoons (1½ sticks) unsalted
   butter, cut into pieces
4 large egg yolks, lightly beaten
1½ teaspoons vanilla extract
2 cups packed sweetened coconut
   flakes
6 ounces pecans, chopped coarse
   (about 1½ cups)

1. *Make the cake:* Position two racks in the top third and center of the oven and preheat to 350°F. Lightly butter the insides of three 9-inch round baking pans. Line the bottoms of the pans with rounds of wax paper. Dust the sides of the pans with flour, tapping out excess.

2. In a small saucepan over low heat, stir the chocolate and boiling water until melted and smooth. Remove from the heat and let cool until tepid, about 10 minutes. Sift the flour, baking soda, and salt together through a wire strainer onto a piece of wax paper.

3. In a large bowl, using a hand-held electric mixer set at high speed, beat the butter until creamy, about 1 minute. Gradually add the sugar and beat until light in color and consistency, about 2 minutes. One at a time, beat in the egg yolks, then the vanilla. Beat in the cooled chocolate mixture. Reduce the mixer speed to low. One-third at a time, alternately beat in the flour mixture and buttermilk, scraping the sides of the bowl with a rubber spatula as necessary.

4. In a medium-size grease-free bowl, using a hand-held electric mixer set at low speed, with clean, dry beaters, beat the egg whites until foamy. Increase the speed to high and beat just until stiff peaks begin to form. Carefully fold the beaten egg whites into the batter. Scrape the batter into the prepared pans, smoothing the tops evenly with the spatula.

5. Place the pans in the oven, arranging them so none of the pans is directly above another or touching another or the sides of the oven. Bake until a toothpick inserted in the center of the cakes comes out clean, 25–30 minutes. Cool on wire cake racks for 15 minutes. Run a sharp knife around the edges of the cakes to loosen them from the sides of the pans. Invert the cakes onto the wire racks, unmold, and carefully remove the wax paper. Turn the cakes right side up and cool completely.

6. *Make the frosting:* In a large saucepan, combine the evaporated milk, sugar, butter, egg yolks, and vanilla. Cook over medium-low heat, stirring constantly with a wooden spoon, until thickened, about 3 minutes. Do not let the mixture come to a boil. Stir in the coconut and pecans. Cool at room temperature, stirring occasionally, until thickened to frosting consistency, about 30 minutes.

7. *Assemble the cake:* Place one cake layer on a serving platter. Using a metal cake spatula, spread the cake with about ⅔ cup of the frosting. Top with a second layer and spread with another ⅔ cup of frosting. Top with the third layer and frost the top and sides of the cake with the remaining frosting. (The cake can be prepared up to 2 days ahead, covered with plastic wrap, and stored at room temperature.)

Makes 8–12 servings

Chocolate Mayonnaise Cake
with Easy Cocoa Frosting

Many of my friends' mothers swear by this 1950s recipe. Despite my skepticism, I decided to give it a try. After thinking about it, I realized the formula isn't odd at all. The eggs and oil in the mayonnaise are found in many cake recipes, and the vinegar seasoning the mayo reacts with the batter's baking soda to work as a leavening agent. This cake is a one-bowl affair, so it's easy to make, and the batter yields tasty black-as-night layers with a firm crumb. It doesn't have as complex a chocolate flavor as more time-consuming cakes, but for a quick recipe it's great! The frosting is also simple, with equally satisfying results.

CAKE
2 cups all-purpose flour
1 cup granulated sugar
⅓ cup plus 1 tablespoon
   nonalkalized cocoa powder, such
   as Hershey's
2 teaspoons baking soda
¼ teaspoon salt
1 cup mayonnaise
1 cup cold strong brewed coffee
1 teaspoon vanilla extract

FROSTING
2½ cups confectioners' sugar
⅔ cup Dutch-process cocoa
   powder, such as Droste
6 tablespoons (¾ stick) unsalted
   butter, softened
¾ cup heavy (whipping) cream
1 teaspoon vanilla extract

1. *Make the cake:* Position a rack in the center of the oven and preheat to 350°F. Lightly butter the insides of two 8-inch round baking pans. Line the bottoms of the pans with rounds of wax paper. Dust the sides of the pans with flour, tapping out excess. Sift the flour, sugar, cocoa, baking soda, and salt together onto a piece of wax paper.

2. In a large bowl, whisk the mayonnaise, coffee, and vanilla until well combined. Add the flour mixture and whisk until smooth. Transfer the batter to the prepared pans and smooth the tops with a rubber spatula.

3. Bake until a toothpick inserted in the center of the cakes comes out clean, 20–25 minutes. Cool the cakes on wire cake racks for 10 minutes. Run a

sharp knife around the inside edges of the pans to loosen the cakes from the sides, then invert the cakes back onto the wire racks. Turn the cakes right side up and cool completely. (The cake layers can be prepared up to 1 day ahead, wrapped in plastic wrap, and stored at room temperature.)

4. *Make the frosting:* Sift the confectioners' sugar and cocoa together through a wire strainer into a medium bowl. In a large bowl, using a hand-held electric mixer set at low speed, beat the butter until creamy. Gradually add the cocoa mixture, alternating it with the heavy cream, beating until the frosting is smooth. (You may have to adjust the amount of cream to reach the desired frosting consistency.) Beat in the vanilla.

5. *Assemble the cake:* Place one cake layer upside down on a serving platter. Using a metal cake spatula, spread about ¾ cup of the frosting evenly onto the layer. Place the second layer right side up on the frosted layer. Evenly frost the top and sides of the cake with the remaining frosting. (The frosted cake can be prepared up to 1 day ahead, covered loosely with plastic wrap, and stored at room temperature.)

Makes 8–10 servings

Chocolate Morsels: For the cake, use natural, nonalkalized cocoa powder (such as Hershey's in the brown box). The baking soda needs the acidity in the natural cocoa to make the cake rise properly. However, for the frosting I prefer Dutch-process cocoa powder (such as Droste or Hershey's in the silver box). Dutch-process cocoa will give the frosting a less bitter cocoa flavor and a deep brown color. You may use nonalkalized cocoa instead if you wish.

Chocolate Pound Cake

I rely on this versatile cake with its fine-grained crumb all year. Try it as the base for sliced strawberries, topped with whipped cream, for an out-of-this-world "shortcake." Serve it with a cold glass of milk for dunking as a satisfying late-night snack. I also use it for Chocolate Raspberry Trifle (see Index).

2½ cups cake flour
½ cup Dutch-process cocoa
   powder, such as Droste
½ teaspoon salt
¼ teaspoon baking soda
1 cup (2 sticks) unsalted butter,
   softened
3 cups granulated sugar
6 large eggs, separated, at room
   temperature
2 teaspoons vanilla or rum extract
1¼ cups sour cream, at room
   temperature

1. Position a rack in the center of the oven and preheat to 350°F. Lightly butter and then flour the inside of a 10-inch tube pan with removable sides, tapping out excess flour. Sift the flour, cocoa, salt, and baking soda together through a wire strainer onto a piece of wax paper.

2. In a large bowl, using a hand-held electric mixer set at high speed, beat the butter until creamy, about 1 minute. Still beating, gradually add the sugar and beat until light in color and consistency, about 2 minutes. One at a time, beat in the egg yolks, beating well after each addition, then the vanilla. A third at a time, alternately add the flour mixture and the sour cream, beating well after each addition and scraping down the sides of the bowl as necessary.

3. In a large grease-free bowl, using a hand-held electric mixer set at low speed, with clean, dry beaters, beat the egg whites until foamy. Increase the speed to medium-high and beat until soft peaks form. Stir about one-fourth

of the beaten egg whites into the batter. Using a rubber spatula, fold in the remaining egg whites. Transfer the batter to the prepared cake pan.

4. Bake until a toothpick inserted in the center of the cake comes out clean, about 1 hour and 20 minutes. Cool on a wire cake rack for 10 minutes.

5. Run a sharp, thin knife around the inside of the pan and the outside of the tube to release the cake. Remove the sides of the cake pan. Slip a metal spatula underneath the cake to release it. Cool completely on a wire cake rack. Using a wide metal spatula as an aid, lift the cake up to remove it from the tube insert and transfer it to a serving plate. (The cake can be prepared up to 2 days ahead, wrapped tightly in plastic wrap and stored at room temperature.)

Makes 10–12 servings

Chocolate Morsels: For a dark chocolate color, use Dutch-process cocoa powder. The alkaline baking soda is used to neutralize the acidity of the sour cream. This is one recipe that calls for baking soda yet doesn't use natural, nonalkalized cocoa powder.

Black and White Layer Cake

This study in contrasts has to be one of the best layer cakes ever. The layers have an extra dose of chocolate flavor, topped with billows of fluffy marshmallow frosting.

CAKE
¾ cup milk
2 teaspoons fresh lemon juice or
  white vinegar
4 ounces unsweetened chocolate,
  chopped fine
¾ cup boiling water
2¼ cups cake flour
1 teaspoon baking soda
¾ teaspoon salt
½ teaspoon baking powder
12 tablespoons (1½ sticks) unsalted
  butter, softened
2 cups granulated sugar
2 large eggs, at room temperature
1 teaspoon vanilla extract

FROSTING
1½ cups granulated sugar
½ cup water
1 tablespoon light corn syrup
3 large egg whites, at room
  temperature
¼ teaspoon salt
1½ teaspoons vanilla extract

1. *Make the cake:* Position a rack in the center of the oven and preheat to 350°F. Lightly butter the insides of two 9-inch round baking pans. Line the bottoms of the pans with rounds of wax paper. Dust the sides of the pans with flour, tapping out excess.

2. In a small measuring cup, combine the milk and lemon juice. Let stand for 10 minutes to curdle the milk. In a small saucepan over very low heat, combine the chocolate and boiling water and melt, stirring constantly. Remove the pan from the heat and let the chocolate mixture cool until tepid, about 10 minutes. Sift the flour, baking soda, salt, and baking powder together through a wire strainer onto a sheet of wax paper.

3. In a large bowl, using a hand-held electric mixer set at high speed, beat the butter until creamy, about 1 minute. Still beating, gradually add the sugar and beat until the mixture is light in color and consistency, about 2

minutes. Beat in the eggs, one at a time, beating well after each addition. Beat in the cooled chocolate and the vanilla.

4. A third at a time, alternately add the dry mixture and curdled milk, beating well after each addition and scraping the sides of the bowl as necessary with a rubber spatula. Transfer the batter to the prepared pans and smooth the tops evenly with the spatula.

5. Bake until a toothpick inserted in the center of the cakes comes out clean, 25–30 minutes. Cool the cakes on wire cake racks for 10 minutes. Run a sharp knife around the edges to loosen cakes from the pan sides. Invert the cakes onto the racks and carefully remove the wax paper. Turn the cakes right side up and cool completely.

6. *Make the frosting:* In a medium saucepan, combine the sugar, water, and corn syrup. Attach a candy thermometer to the pan, making sure it does not touch the bottom. Cook over medium-high heat, stirring constantly, until the mixture comes to a boil. Wash down any crystals on the side of the saucepan with a pastry brush dipped in cold water. Without stirring, continue to boil the mixture over medium-high heat until the thermometer reads 240°F.

7. In a large grease-free bowl, using a hand-held electric mixer set at low speed, with clean, dry beaters, beat the egg whites until foamy. Add the salt, increase the speed to medium-high, and continue beating just until soft peaks form. Gradually beat in the syrup and continue beating for 6–8 minutes, until the frosting has cooled and stiff, shiny peaks form. Beat in the vanilla.

8. *Assemble the cake:* Place a cake layer upside down on a platter. Using a metal cake spatula, frost the layer with about ½ cup of the frosting. Place the second layer right side up on the frosted layer. Frost the top and sides of the cake with the remaining frosting, swirling the frosting on the top of the cake.

Makes 8 servings

Chocolate Morsels: When you are beating the frosting, place the bowl on a wire cake rack to increase air circulation underneath the bowl. This way the frosting will cool to the proper spreading temperature more quickly.

To make Peppermint Black and White Cake, stir ½ cup finely crushed peppermint candies into the cooled beaten frosting.

Beware of making the frosting on humid days—it will not beat properly and will be too sticky to frost with.

Cocoa Angel Food Cake
with Strawberry Whip

My family always looks forward to strawberry season, because that means Mom will be making her feather-light angel food cake with a fluffy whipped cream frosting, made pink with sweetened chopped berries. But, as with many heirloom desserts that seem deceptively simple, there are a few little tricks to making perfect angel food cake, and they are outlined throughout the recipe. Not just for nostalgia's sake, this is one of my favorite desserts. Serve it chilled with more sliced berries on the side if you like.

CAKE
1¼ cups superfine sugar, divided
¾ cup cake flour
¼ cup Dutch-process cocoa
    powder, such as Droste
12 large egg whites, at room
    temperature
1 teaspoon cream of tartar
¼ teaspoon salt
1 teaspoon vanilla extract

STRAWBERRY WHIP
1 pint fresh strawberries, hulled
    and chopped coarse
3 tablespoons confectioners' sugar,
    divided
1 cup heavy (whipping) cream

1 pint fresh strawberries, hulled
    and sliced, for garnish

1. *Make the cake:* Position a rack in the center of the oven and preheat to 350°F. *Do not butter or flour* a 10-inch round tube pan with removable sides. Greasing the pan will inhibit the batter from clinging to the pan and properly rising. Sift ¾ cup of the superfine sugar, the cake flour, and the cocoa together through a wire strainer onto a piece of wax paper.

2. In a large grease-free bowl, using a hand-held electric mixer set at low speed, with clean, dry beaters, beat the egg whites until very foamy, about 30 seconds. Add the cream of tartar and salt. Increase the speed to medium-high and continue beating, gradually adding the remaining ½ cup of superfine sugar, just until the whites form stiff peaks. Do not overbeat the whites. Add the vanilla, which will be folded in with the flour.

3. A third at a time, resift the flour mixture over the beaten whites and fold together, using a balloon whisk or a rubber spatula. Transfer the batter to the ungreased 10-inch round tube pan and smooth the top evenly with the rubber spatula.

4. Bake for about 60 minutes, until the cake has risen and a long bamboo skewer inserted in the center comes out clean. Completely cool the cake upside down. The cake must clear the counter—balance the edges of the pan on three equally spaced coffee mugs if necessary. Cooling will take at least 4 hours or overnight. (The cake can be prepared up to 2 days ahead, wrapped tightly in plastic wrap, and stored at room temperature.)

5. *Make the strawberry whip:* In a medium bowl, combine the chopped strawberries with 1 tablespoon of the confectioners' sugar. Cover and refrigerate until the strawberries give off their juices, about 2 hours. Drain the strawberries, reserving the juices.

6. In a chilled medium bowl, whip the cream just until soft peaks begin to form. Add the drained strawberries and the remaining 2 tablespoons of confectioners' sugar and beat just until stiff.

7. *Assemble the cake:* Run a sharp, thin knife around the inside edge and tube of the cake pan. Invert the pan and remove the sides. Carefully cut the bottom of the cake from the bottom of the tube insert and remove the cake.

8. Place the cake on a serving platter. Drizzle the top with the reserved juices. Frost the cake with the strawberry whip. Refrigerate the cake, covered loosely with plastic wrap, until ready to serve, up to 1 day. Slice the cake with a serrated knife and garnish each serving with the sliced strawberries.

Makes 8–10 servings

Chocolate Zucchini Cake

For those of us with overproductive summer gardens this recipe is a godsend. Others may be skeptical about such an odd-sounding combination. But believe me, many a county fair blue ribbon has been awarded to vegetable-chocolate cakes. I've baked chocolate-sauerkraut, chocolate-beet, and chocolate-carrot cakes, and all were delicious. But this moist, walnut-studded zucchini cake is my choice for best of show.

2½ cups all-purpose flour
½ cup Dutch-process cocoa
    powder, such as Droste
2½ teaspoons baking powder
1½ teaspoons baking soda
1 teaspoon salt
1 teaspoon ground cinnamon
12 tablespoons (1½ sticks) unsalted
    butter, at room temperature
2¼ cups granulated sugar
3 large eggs, at room temperature
2 teaspoons vanilla extract
Grated zest of 1 large orange
½ cup milk
2 cups (about ¾ pound, 2–3
    medium) coarsely grated
    zucchini
4 ounces walnuts, toasted (see
    Index) and chopped coarse
    (about 1 cup)
Confectioners' sugar, for garnish

1. Position a rack in the center of the oven and preheat to 350°F. Lightly butter and then flour the inside of a 10-inch round tube pan with removable sides, tapping out the excess flour. Sift the flour, cocoa, baking powder, baking soda, salt, and cinnamon together through a wire strainer onto a piece of wax paper.

2. In a large bowl, using a hand-held electric mixer set at high speed, beat the butter until creamy, about 1 minute. Gradually add the sugar and beat until light in color and consistency, about 2 minutes. One at a time, beat in the eggs, beating well after each addition. Beat in the vanilla and orange zest. A third at a time, alternately add the flour mixture and milk, beating well after each addition and scraping down the sides of the bowl as necessary. (The batter will be thick.) Stir in the zucchini and nuts. Transfer the batter to the prepared pan, smoothing the top with a rubber spatula.

3. Bake until a toothpick inserted in the center of the cake comes out clean, about 1 hour. Cool on a wire cake rack for 10 minutes.

4. Run a sharp, thin knife around the inside of the pan and the outside of the tube to release the cake. Remove the sides of the pan. Slip a metal spatula underneath the cake to release it. Let the cake cool completely on a wire cake rack.

5. Using a wide, flat spatula as an aid, lift the cake up to remove it from the tube insert and transfer it to a serving plate. Sift confectioners' sugar over the top of the cake before serving. (The cake can be prepared up to 2 days ahead, covered with plastic wrap, and stored at room temperature.)

Makes 8–12 servings

Chocolate-Buttermilk Snackin' Cake

This thin, flavor-packed sheet cake with a slightly tangy chocolate frosting has so much going for it, I don't know where to start. The cake is prepared in a snap, doesn't even call for an electric mixer, and is baked in a jelly-roll pan. This is one of my most popular recipes for big get-togethers, because it makes enough for a small army and is easy to transport to picnics and other gatherings.

CAKE
2 cups all-purpose flour
2 cups granulated sugar
1 teaspoon baking soda
¼ teaspoon salt
8 tablespoons (1 stick) unsalted
   butter, cut into pieces
1 cup water
¼ cup nonalkalized cocoa powder,
   such as Hershey's
½ teaspoon instant coffee powder
2 large eggs, beaten
⅓ cup buttermilk
1 teaspoon vanilla extract

ICING
8 tablespoons (1 stick) unsalted
   butter, cut into pieces
⅓ cup buttermilk
¼ cup nonalkalized cocoa powder,
   such as Hershey's
1 pound confectioners' sugar,
   sifted
4 ounces walnuts, toasted (see
   Index) and chopped coarse
   (about 1 cup)
1 teaspoon vanilla extract

1. *Make the cake:* Position a rack in the center of the oven and preheat to 400°F. Lightly butter the bottom and sides of a 17″ × 11″ jelly-roll pan.

2. Sift the flour, sugar, baking soda, and salt together through a wire strainer into a large bowl. In a medium saucepan, bring the butter, water, and cocoa to a boil over high heat. Remove the pan from the heat, add the coffee powder, and whisk until smooth. Pour the cocoa mixture into the dry ingredients and whisk until combined.

3. In a small bowl, whisk together the eggs, buttermilk, and vanilla. Add to the batter and whisk until smooth. Transfer to the prepared pan and smooth evenly.

30

4. Bake until the cake springs back when pressed lightly in the center with a finger, 12–15 minutes. Transfer the pan to a wire cake rack and cool the cake slightly, about 5 minutes.

5. *Make the icing:* As soon as the cake comes out of the oven, bring the butter, buttermilk, and cocoa to a boil in a medium saucepan over medium-high heat, whisking occasionally until combined. Remove the pan from the heat and stir in the confectioners' sugar, walnuts, and vanilla until smooth.

6. Using a metal cake spatula, preferably offset, carefully spread the icing over the warm cake. Let the cake cool completely at room temperature until the icing is set. (The cake can be prepared up to 1 day ahead, covered tightly with plastic wrap, and stored at room temperature.)

Makes 12–16 servings

The Ultimate Devil's Food Cake with Fudgy Frosting

Although it is sinfully good, devil's food cake is actually named for its crumb's devilish, brick-red tint. (It's baking soda reacting with the chocolate that gives the distinctive coloring.) I am very proud of my version, which avoids many of the pitfalls of less "ultimate" recipes that can have an "off" taste and an artificial color. I believe that a true devil's food cake should be leavened only with baking soda, so there isn't a bit of baking powder in my version. However, it must not have the overly "soapy" flavor that some cakes get when they overdo the baking soda. It should have a reddish tinge, without, heaven forbid, ever getting any help from the food coloring bottle. My guests declared this cake, slathered with fudge frosting, hands down, the best old-fashioned chocolate cake they'd enjoyed since Grandma's.

CAKE
3 ounces unsweetened chocolate, chopped fine
2 cups cake flour
1¼ teaspoons baking soda
½ teaspoon salt
8 tablespoons (1 stick) unsalted butter, softened
1½ cups granulated sugar
2 large eggs, at room temperature
1 teaspoon vanilla extract
1¼ cups buttermilk

FROSTING
2 cups granulated sugar
⅔ cup milk
8 tablespoons (1 stick) unsalted butter, cut into pieces
3 ounces unsweetened chocolate, chopped fine
1 tablespoon light corn syrup
¼ teaspoon salt
2 teaspoons vanilla extract

1. *Make the cake:* Position a rack in the center of the oven and preheat to 350°F. Lightly butter the insides of two 9-inch round baking pans. Line the bottoms of the pans with rounds of wax paper. Dust the sides of the pans with flour and tap out excess.

2. In the top part of a double boiler over hot, not simmering, water, melt the chocolate, stirring often until smooth. Remove the top pan from the bottom and let the chocolate cool, stirring often, until tepid, about 10 minutes.

3. Sift the flour, baking soda, and salt together through a wire strainer onto a piece of wax paper. In a medium bowl, using a hand-held electric mixer set at high speed, beat the butter until creamy, about 1 minute. Gradually add the sugar and beat until light in color and consistency, about 2 minutes. One at a time, beat in the eggs, then the vanilla. Beat in the cooled chocolate. One third at a time, alternately add the flour mixture and the buttermilk, beating well after each addition and scraping down the sides of the bowl. Transfer the batter to the prepared pans, smoothing the tops with a rubber spatula.

4. Bake until a toothpick inserted in the center of the cakes comes out clean, 22–27 minutes. Cool the cakes on wire cake racks for 10 minutes. Run a sharp knife around the edges of the cakes to loosen them from the pans, then invert the cakes onto wire cake racks. Carefully remove the wax paper, turn the cakes right side up, and cool the cakes completely. (The cake layers can be prepared 1 day ahead, wrapped in plastic wrap, and stored at room temperature. They can also be frozen, wrapped tightly in plastic wrap and then aluminum foil, for up to 1 month.)

5. *Make the frosting:* In a heavy-bottomed medium saucepan, combine the sugar, milk, butter, chocolate, corn syrup, and salt. Bring to a boil over medium-high heat, stirring constantly with a wooden spoon to dissolve the sugar. When the mixture comes to a boil, stop stirring and cook for 1 minute. Remove from the heat and stir in the vanilla.

6. Place the saucepan in a large bowl of ice. Let the frosting mixture stand, stirring often with a wooden spoon, until cool and thickened. As the mixture cools, be sure to scrape the thickened, cooled mixture on the bottom and sides of the pan into the rest of the frosting. When cool, remove the bowl from the ice and beat well with the wooden spoon until the frosting is smooth and spreadable, about 3 minutes. Frost the cake without delay.

7. *Assemble the cake:* Place one cake layer upside down on a serving platter. Using a metal cake spatula, spread about ¾ cup of the frosting evenly onto the layer. Place the second layer right side up on the frosted layer. Frost the top and sides of the cake with the remaining frosting. If the frosting becomes difficult to spread, use a hot, wet cake spatula. (The frosted cake can be prepared up to 1 day ahead, covered with plastic wrap, and stored at room temperature.)

Makes 8 servings

Wicky Wacky Chocolate Cake

You may be familiar with similar "one-bowl wonder" recipes with different names—Three-in-One Cake, Amazing Cake, and so on. In spite of the fact that the cake contains no eggs, it rises to moist, yummy heights. (The chemical reaction between the acidic cocoa and vinegar and the alkaline baking soda gives the cake its impressive leavening power.) Because this is supposed to be a lazy-day dessert, I rarely bother to make a bona fide frosting. Simply dust the top with lots of confectioners' sugar or serve the cake with dollops of lightly sweetened whipped cream, as I do here.

3 cups all-purpose flour
2 cups granulated sugar
½ cup nonalkalized cocoa powder,
    such as Hershey's
2 teaspoons baking soda
¾ teaspoon salt
¾ cup vegetable oil
2 tablespoons cider vinegar
2 teaspoons vanilla extract
2 cups milk
1 cup heavy (whipping) cream
    (optional)
2 tablespoons confectioners' sugar
    (optional)

1. Position a rack in the center of the oven and preheat to 350°F. Lightly butter and then flour a 9″ × 13″ baking pan, tapping out excess flour.

2. Sift the flour, sugar, cocoa, baking soda, and salt together into a large bowl. Make three wells in the dry ingredients. Individually, place the vegetable oil, vinegar, and vanilla in the wells. Pour the milk over the mixture. Using a wooden spoon, stir together just until well blended. Scrape the batter into the prepared pan.

3. Bake until a toothpick inserted in the center of the cake comes out clean, 25–30 minutes. Cool completely in the pan on a wire cake rack.

4. If desired, in a chilled medium bowl, using a hand-held electric mixer set at high speed, beat the cream just until soft peaks begin to form. Beat in the confectioners' sugar. Serve the cake with the whipped cream.

Makes 10–12 servings

Chocolate Morsels: It is very important to use a natural, nonalkalized cocoa, such as Hershey's (in the brown box). A Dutch-process cocoa (such as Droste or Hershey's European-Style in the silver box) will not react properly with baking soda, and the cake will rise unevenly—to say nothing of the undesirable soapy flavor that will result.

If desired, stir 1 cup semisweet chocolate chips or toasted walnut pieces into the batter before baking.

On *very* lazy days you can mix the batter right in the pan. In this case, lightly butter the inside of the pan, but do not flour it. Sift the dry ingredients directly into the pan and proceed, being sure to mix into the corners of the pan. I think the mixing is much more efficient in a bowl.

One of the pleasures of this cake (without the whipped cream topping) is that it is very low in cholesterol, with no eggs and no butter and a minimum of milk per serving. It is the perfect chocolate dessert to serve, topped with lots of fresh berries, to guests concerned about cholesterol. However, you may also choose to substitute 12 tablespoons (1½ sticks) unsalted butter, melted, for the vegetable oil.

Orange-Chocolate Bundt Cake

At least once a year my friend Marie makes me one of her incredible Grand Marnier cakes. I decided that if her version was so spectacular I would go one step further and "chocolatize" it. The result was extraordinary. (P.S. Marie prefers her original version, since she is allergic to chocolate.)

CAKE
3 ounces unsweetened chocolate, chopped fine
2 cups all-purpose flour
1½ teaspoons baking soda
½ teaspoon baking powder
½ teaspoon salt
8 tablespoons (1 stick) unsalted butter, softened
1½ cups granulated sugar
3 large eggs, at room temperature
1½ teaspoons vanilla extract
Grated zest of 1 large orange (save orange for syrup)
1¼ cups sour cream, at room temperature
1 6-ounce package (about 1 cup) semisweet chocolate chips

ORANGE SYRUP
½ cup Grand Marnier or other orange-flavored liqueur
Juice of 1 large orange
⅓ cup superfine sugar

GLAZE
4 tablespoons (½ stick) unsalted butter, cut into pieces
4 ounces semisweet chocolate, chopped fine
1 tablespoon light corn syrup

1. *Make the cake:* Position a rack in the center of the oven and preheat to 350°F. Lightly butter and then flour the inside of a 12-cup fluted tube pan, such as Bundt, and tap out excess flour.

2. In the top part of a double boiler set over hot, not simmering, water, melt the chocolate, stirring often, until smooth. Remove the top part of the double boiler from the bottom and cool the chocolate, stirring often, until tepid, about 10 minutes.

3. Sift the flour, baking soda, baking powder, and salt together through a wire strainer onto a piece of wax paper. In a medium bowl, using a hand-held electric mixer set at high speed, beat the butter until creamy, about 1 minute. Still beating, gradually add the sugar and beat until light in color and consistency, about 2 minutes. One at a time, beat in the eggs, then the vanilla and orange zest. Beat in the cooled chocolate. A third at a time, alternately beat in the flour mixture and the sour cream, beating well after each addition and scraping down the sides of the bowl as necessary. Stir in the chocolate chips. Transfer the batter to the prepared pan and smooth the top with the spatula.

4. Bake until a toothpick inserted in the center of the cake comes out clean, 50–60 minutes. Place the cake on a wire cake rack but do not remove from pan.

5. *Make the syrup:* In a small bowl, whisk together the liqueur, orange juice, and sugar until the sugar is dissolved. Slowly pour the syrup over the top of the cake. Let the cake cool for 10 minutes. Invert the cake onto the wire cake rack and cool completely.

6. *Make the glaze:* In a small saucepan, melt the butter over medium heat. Remove the saucepan from the heat and add the chocolate and corn syrup. Let the mixture stand until the chocolate is melted, about 2 minutes, then whisk until smooth. Let the glaze stand until thickened but still pourable, about 15 minutes.

7. Drizzle the glaze over the top of the cake, letting the excess run down the sides. Refrigerate the cake until the glaze is set, about 15 minutes. (The cake can be prepared up to 2 days before serving, wrapped in plastic wrap, and stored at room temperature.)

Makes 10–12 servings

Banana-Chocolate Loaf Cake

Wait until you smell the mingling aromas of chocolate, bananas, and walnuts baking in your oven! This ultramoist loaf cake has become one of my favorites. You can serve it around the clock, as a special sweet for a weekend breakfast, a quick afternoon pick-me-up, or even a dinnertime dessert, adorned with a scoop of vanilla ice cream and homemade fudge sauce (see Index).

1 ounce unsweetened chocolate,
   chopped fine
½ cup milk
1 teaspoon fresh lemon juice
2 cups all-purpose flour
2 tablespoons Dutch-process cocoa
   powder, such as Droste
¾ teaspoon baking soda
½ teaspoon baking powder
¼ teaspoon salt
8 tablespoons (1 stick) unsalted
   butter, softened
1½ cups granulated sugar
2 large eggs, at room temperature
1 cup (about 2 medium) mashed
   ripe bananas
1 teaspoon vanilla extract
4 ounces walnuts, toasted (see
   Index) and chopped coarse
   (about 1 cup)

1. Position a rack in the center of the oven and preheat to 350°F. Lightly butter the inside of a 9″ × 5″ × 3″ loaf pan. Line the bottom of the pan with wax paper. Dust the sides of the pan with flour, tapping out excess.

2. In the top part of a double boiler over hot, not simmering, water, melt the chocolate, stirring often, until smooth. Remove the top part of the pan

from the heat and let the chocolate cool, stirring often, until tepid, about 10 minutes.

3. In a glass measuring cup, combine the milk and lemon juice and let stand for 10 minutes, until curdled. Sift the flour, cocoa, baking soda, baking powder, and salt together through a wire strainer onto a piece of wax paper.

4. In a large bowl, using a hand-held electric mixer set at high speed, beat the butter until creamy, about 1 minute. Still beating, gradually add the sugar and beat until light in color and consistency, about 2 minutes. One at a time, beat in the eggs. Add the cooled chocolate, mashed bananas, and vanilla and beat until smooth. Stir in walnuts. Reduce the mixer speed to low. A third at a time, alternately add the flour mixture and the milk mixture, beating well after each addition and scraping down the sides of the bowl as necessary. Transfer the batter to the prepared pan, smoothing the top with a rubber spatula.

5. Bake until a toothpick inserted in the center of the pan comes out clean, 70–80 minutes. Let the cake cool in the pan on a wire cake rack for 20 minutes. Run a sharp knife around the inside edges of the pan to release the cake from the sides. Invert and unmold the cake onto a wire cake rack and carefully peel off the wax paper. Invert the cake again, so it is right side up, and cool completely. (The cake can be prepared up to 1 day ahead, wrapped tightly in plastic wrap, and stored at room temperature.)

Makes about 8 servings

Chocolate Morsels: Be sure the bananas are very ripe. Buy them 4–5 days ahead to be sure they are mottled with plenty of brown spots before mashing, or even a couple of days longer, until the bananas are black-ripe and very soft.

Be sure to use Dutch-process cocoa powder (such as Droste or Hershey's European-Style in the silver box) in this recipe. Otherwise the leavening will be affected.

6
Star-Spangled Sweets

❧

Make-It-Easy Chocolate Fudge
Classic Fudge
Macadamia Milk Chocolate Crunch
Chocolate–Peanut Butter Meltaways
My Dad's Famous Rocky Road
Peanut Butter and Milk Chocolate Brownies
Blondies with Chocolate Chunks
Lois's Brownies
Kiss Kookies
Texas Pecan and Chocolate Toffee Cookies
Cakey Chocolate Chip–Raisin Cookies
Chewy Chocolate and White Chocolate Chip Cookies
Diane's Triple-Layered Delights
Impossible Dream Bars
Chocolate-Raisin Bread Pudding
Chocolate Peanut Pie
Mississippi Mud Cake
Chocolate Swirl Cheesecake with Chocolate-Nut Crust
Chocolate Cranberry Cheesecake

Make-It-Easy Chocolate Fudge

Happy memories of my family's holiday candy dish include Grandma's vanilla-walnut divinity (which, alas, was chocolateless and so cannot be included here), My Dad's Famous Rocky Road (see Index), and our friend Rose's fudge. Here's Rose's candy, with my clarifications, based on a well-used, dog-eared recipe written in her own hand.

8 tablespoons (1 stick) unsalted
 butter, cut into pieces
1 6-ounce package (about 1 cup)
 semisweet chocolate chips
4 ounces walnuts, toasted (see
 Index) and chopped coarse
 (about 1 cup)
1 ounce unsweetened chocolate,
 chopped fine
1 teaspoon vanilla extract
2¼ cups granulated sugar
1 5-ounce can evaporated milk
3 ounces large marshmallows
 (about 12)

1. Line a 9-inch square baking pan with a double thickness of aluminum foil so that the foil extends 2 inches over the opposite ends of the pan. Fold the overhang down to form handles. Butter the inside of the foil-lined pan.

2. In a large bowl, combine the butter, chocolate chips, walnuts, unsweetened chocolate, and vanilla.

3. In a large, heavy-bottomed saucepan, combine the sugar, evaporated milk, and marshmallows. Lightly butter the exposed inside of the saucepan above the surface of the sugar mixture. Bring to a boil over medium heat, stirring constantly with a flat wooden spatula to prevent scorching. Attach a

candy thermometer to the pan, making sure it does not touch the bottom. Boil, stirring constantly, until the thermometer reaches 238°F (soft ball stage).

4. Pour the evaporated milk mixture over the ingredients in the bowl. Let stand for 30 seconds and then stir until the mixture thickens and begins to lose its sheen, about 1 minute. Spread the mixture evenly in the prepared pan. Let stand at room temperature until completely cooled and the flavors have mellowed, at least overnight.

5. Lift up the foil "handles" to remove the fudge from the pan. Using a sharp knife, cut the fudge into squares and lift it from the foil. (The fudge can be prepared up to 1 week ahead and stored in an airtight container at room temperature.)

Makes about 2¼ pounds

Chocolate Morsels: Because it is supposedly "fail-proof," marshmallow-based fudge is a standard in many candy cooks' recipe boxes. But that does not mean you can't botch a batch, as I once did, even though I followed Rose's directions to the letter. The problem was that she simply said to boil the evaporated milk syrup for 6 minutes, without mentioning a candy thermometer reading. One man's boil is another man's simmer; my syrup wasn't cooked enough at 6 minutes, and my fudge flopped. For the second batch I cooked it to 238°F, the accepted temperature for fudge, and success was mine. If you have an old family recipe that gives only a boiling time, remember to boil the syrup to the soft ball stage, regardless of the time it takes.

Classic Fudge

Hail to the legendary ladies of Vassar and Wellesley Colleges, who, according to a tale every chocolate lover knows by heart, made batches of fudge in their dormitory rooms by the heat of a Bunsen burner. Real fudge is easy to make, but you need to pay a little attention to detail to avoid an overly grainy end result. In this time-honored recipe I will guide you to fudgy perfection.

2 cups granulated sugar
1 cup half-and-half
2 ounces unsweetened chocolate,
   chopped coarse
2 tablespoons light corn syrup
⅛ teaspoon salt
2 tablespoons unsalted butter,
   chilled
1 teaspoon vanilla extract

1. Lightly butter the inside of a 9″ × 5″ loaf pan. Attach a candy thermometer to a small saucepan of water, making sure the thermometer doesn't touch the bottom of the pan, and bring to a boil. Remove the pan from the heat and set aside with the thermometer still attached. (See Chocolate Morsels.)

2. Lightly butter the inside of a heavy-bottomed medium saucepan with at least a 2½-quart capacity. Add the sugar, half-and-half, chocolate, corn syrup, and salt. Bring to a boil over high heat, stirring constantly to dissolve the sugar.

3. As soon as the mixture comes to a boil, stop stirring and attach the hot candy thermometer to the saucepan, making sure the thermometer does not touch the bottom of the pan. Reduce the heat to medium. Cook, stirring occasionally with a wooden spoon to prevent scorching on the bottom of the pan, until the candy thermometer reads about 240°F (soft ball stage), 10–15 minutes.

4. Immediately place the saucepan in a large bowl of cold water. Add the butter and vanilla, but do not stir in. Let the fudge cool, without stirring,

until the thermometer reads 110°F and a skin forms on the surface, about 20 minutes.

5. Remove the pan from the water. Using a sturdy wooden spoon, stir the fudge until it thickens, loses its sheen, and holds its shape when you stop stirring, about 5 minutes.

6. Immediately pour the fudge into the prepared pan. Cool completely at room temperature until firm. Do not refrigerate. The fudge tastes best if allowed to mellow overnight. Using a sharp, thin knife, cut the fudge into pieces. Turn the pan upside down to release the fudge. (The fudge can be prepared up to 2 weeks ahead and stored in an airtight container at room temperature.)

Makes about 1½ pounds

Chocolate Morsels: Preheating your candy thermometer in boiling water gives a more accurate reading. Check your thermometer's accuracy in the boiling water—it should read 212°F. If it doesn't, just adjust your temperature readings according to the variance. For example, if your thermometer reads 208°F in boiling water, it is 4°F off, so add 4°F to your fudge-boiling temperature (244°F).

Buttering the sides of the pan prevents sugar crystals from forming in your fudge mixture. If crystals form, wash them off the sides of the pan with a pastry brush dipped in water.

To make Chocolate Nut Fudge, place 4 ounces walnuts or pecans, chopped coarse (about 1 cup), in the bottom of the loaf pan and pour the stirred fudge directly onto the nuts. If you try to stir the nuts into the fudge, they may cause your fudge to harden too quickly to pour.

You may vary the flavor of your fudge by substituting ½ teaspoon flavoring extract (such as peppermint, rum, or coconut) for the vanilla. (You use less of the other flavoring extracts than vanilla because they're stronger.)

Never try to make fudge on a humid day. The moisture in the air will make the candy grainy. If you must have fudge, use the recipe for Make-It-Easy Chocolate Fudge (see Index).

Macadamia Milk Chocolate Crunch

Buttery English toffee goes Hawaiian with the addition of macadamia nuts. Presented in a colorful tin, it is the perfect way to say "aloha" the next time you are a weekend guest.

2 cups granulated sugar
1½ cups (3 sticks) unsalted butter,
    cut into pieces
4 ounces macadamia nuts, rinsed
    of salt, patted dry, and chopped
    coarse (about 1 cup)
¼ teaspoon baking soda, sifted to
    remove lumps
6 ounces milk chocolate, chopped
    coarse

1. Lightly butter a 10″ × 15″ baking sheet. In a heavy-bottomed large saucepan, combine the sugar and butter. Cook over medium-high heat, stirring constantly, until the mixture comes to a boil.

2. Attach a candy thermometer to the pan, making sure it does not touch the bottom, and continue to cook the mixture over medium-high heat, stirring constantly, until the thermometer reads 278°F (hard crack stage).

3. Remove the pan from the heat and stir in the nuts and baking soda. Pour the mixture evenly into the prepared pan. Let the toffee stand for 5 minutes to cool slightly.

4. Sprinkle the milk chocolate in a single layer over the surface of the toffee. Let stand until the chocolate is softened, about 5 minutes. Using an offset metal spatula, spread the chocolate evenly over the surface of the toffee. With a large sharp knife, score the toffee into 35 2-inch squares. As the toffee cools, retrace the score lines with the knife occasionally to reach the bottom of the pan so the toffee will break apart easily.

5. When the milk chocolate is firm and the toffee is completely cooled, use a metal spatula to remove the toffee from the pan. Following the score lines, break it into chunks and serve. (The toffee can be made up to 1 week ahead and stored in an airtight container at cool room temperature.)

Makes about 35 pieces

Chocolate Morsels: Just about any unsalted nut would be delicious here. Cashews, peanuts, and walnuts are fine. Try using bittersweet or semisweet instead of milk chocolate for a wonderful change.

Chocolate-Peanut Butter Meltaways

I'll never forget the Christmas my friend Marian visited and her mother, Catherine, sent us a box of her handmade Chocolate-Peanut Butter Meltaways. It was love at first bite—crunchy, chocolaty, nutty. By the second mouthful I was on the phone with Catherine getting the recipe!

9 ounces bittersweet chocolate,
    chopped coarse
2 tablespoons vegetable shortening
1 12-ounce jar crunchy peanut
    butter
5 tablespoons unsalted butter at
    room temperature
2 cups confectioners' sugar, sifted
1½ cups crispy rice cereal

1. In the top part of a double boiler set over hot, not simmering, water, melt the chocolate and vegetable shortening, stirring often, until smooth. Remove the top part of the double boiler from the bottom. Transfer the chocolate mixture to a small bowl and cool slightly, stirring often.

2. Meanwhile, in a medium bowl, using a wooden spoon, cream the peanut butter and butter until well combined. Gradually add the confectioners' sugar and mix until smooth. Stir in the cereal, which will crumble. Press about 1 tablespoon of the mixture between your fingertips and roll it between your palms to form a smooth ball. Transfer the ball to a wax paper–lined baking sheet. Repeat with the remaining mixture.

3. Line a baking sheet with aluminum foil and place it next to the bowl of melted chocolate. With one hand, tilt the bowl so the chocolate forms a pool almost level with the rim of the bowl. With the other hand, place a peanut butter ball on the surface of the chocolate. Using a professional three-pronged candy fork or a regular fork, press down on the peanut butter ball so that the sides are submerged in the chocolate mixture. Turn the ball over to coat completely. Using the fork, lift the coated ball out of the chocolate mixture.

Gently tap the fork on the side of the bowl and scrape the fork along the rim of the bowl to remove any excess chocolate. Place the coated ball on the prepared baking sheet. Continue the process with the remaining balls and chocolate.

4. Refrigerate the balls until the chocolate is set and the balls release easily from the foil, about 30 minutes. (The candies can be prepared up to 1 week ahead, stored in an airtight container, and refrigerated.)

Makes about 45 candies

My Dad's Famous Rocky Road

Every year at Christmastime, my dad makes pound after pound of this fabulous treat. (Dad says, "I've never made Rocky Road with any other kind of chocolate than Hershey's, or marshmallows other than Kraft's, and I don't care to try it otherwise. Why fool with perfection?" Amen, Dad.) It is a "no muss, no fuss" kind of candy that guys like to prepare. If you have a young son who is itching to try his hand in the kitchen, check this out. Your daughter will like it too.

> 1 pound milk chocolate, chopped
>   coarse
> 8 ounces large marshmallows, cut
>   into fourths
> 4 ounces walnuts, toasted (see
>   Index) and crushed coarse
>   (about 1 cup)

1. In the top part of a double boiler set over hot, not simmering, water, heat the chocolate, stirring occasionally, until almost melted. Remove the top part of the double boiler from the bottom and cool the chocolate, stirring often, until all the chocolate is melted and tepid.

2. Lightly butter a baking sheet. Stir the marshmallows and nuts into the tepid chocolate until well combined. (Stir a couple of marshmallows into the chocolate as a test. If they melt, the chocolate is too hot and needs to be cooled longer. If the rocky road becomes hard and too stiff to stir, heat gently over hot water until the chocolate melts slightly.)

3. Spoon the mixture onto the baking sheet. Refrigerate until firm, at least 4 hours. Using a sharp knife, cut into squares. (The rocky road can be prepared up to 2 weeks ahead and stored in an airtight container.)

Makes about 1¾ pounds

Peanut Butter and Milk Chocolate Brownies

Of all flavor combinations, what is more quintessentially American than peanut butter and milk chocolate? These brownies put me in mind of dime-store candy bars—the brown sugar gives the bars a chewy, caramel character that is the perfect mate for the milk chocolate icing. Luckily this recipe makes a large batch, because these brownies will disappear quickly from your cookie jar.

1 cup crunchy peanut butter
10 tablespoons (1¼ sticks) unsalted butter, softened
1 teaspoon vanilla extract
2 cups packed light brown sugar
3 large eggs, at room temperature

1 cup all-purpose flour
½ teaspoon salt
½ cup (about 3 ounces) semisweet chocolate chips
6 ounces milk chocolate bars, chopped coarse

1. Position a rack in the center of the oven and preheat to 350°F. Lightly butter and then flour a 9″ × 13″ baking pan, tapping out excess flour.

2. In a medium bowl, using a hand-held electric mixer set at medium-high speed, cream together the peanut butter, butter, and vanilla until well combined, about 1 minute. Gradually add the brown sugar and beat until light in color and consistency, about 2 minutes. Beat in the eggs, one at a time, beating well after each addition. Using a wooden spoon, stir in the flour and salt. Stir in the chocolate chips. Spread the batter evenly into the prepared pan.

3. Bake until a toothpick inserted in the center comes out clean, 18–22 minutes. Cool slightly in the pan on a wire cake rack, about 5 minutes.

4. Sprinkle the milk chocolate over the surface of the warm brownies. Let the milk chocolate stand until softened, about 5 minutes. Using a metal cake spatula, spread the milk chocolate evenly over the brownies. Cool the brownies completely, refrigerating the brownies to set the icing if necessary. (The brownies can be prepared up to 2 days ahead, wrapped individually in plastic wrap, and stored at room temperature.)

Makes about 28 brownies

Blondies with Chocolate Chunks

I've always contended that vanilla and chocolate are old friends, not rivals, since they "grew up" side by side in the Central American jungles for aeons before the Spaniards exported them both to the New World. Therefore, I feel no remorse for the times when I indulge in a butterscotch-flavored blondie (albeit studded with chocolate chunks) instead of a brownie.

2 cups all-purpose flour
1 teaspoon salt
1 teaspoon baking powder
¼ teaspoon baking soda
10 tablespoons (1¼ sticks) unsalted
    butter, softened
2 cups packed light brown sugar
2 large eggs, at room temperature
2 teaspoons vanilla extract
6 ounces bittersweet chocolate, cut
    into ½-inch square chunks
4 ounces pecans, toasted (see
    Index) and chopped coarse
    (about 1 cup)

1. Position a rack in the center of the oven and preheat to 350°F. Line a 9″ × 13″ baking pan with a double thickness of aluminum foil so that the foil extends beyond the two opposite ends of the pan. Fold the overhang down to form handles. Lightly butter the bottom and sides of the foil-lined pan. Dust the insides of the pan with flour, tapping out excess. Sift the flour, salt, baking powder, and baking soda together through a wire strainer onto a sheet of wax paper.

2. In a medium bowl, using a hand-held electric mixer set at high speed, beat the butter until creamy, about 1 minute. Gradually beat in the brown sugar and beat until light in color and consistency, about 2 minutes. One at a time, beat in the eggs, beating well after each addition. Beat in the vanilla.

Using a wooden spoon, stir in the flour mixture. Stir in the chocolate chunks and nuts. Transfer the batter to the prepared pan, spreading evenly and smoothing the top with a metal cake spatula.

3. Bake until a toothpick inserted in the center of the blondies comes out with a moist crumb, 25–30 minutes. *Do not overbake.* Cool completely in the pan on a wire cake rack.

4. Run a knife around the inside edges of the pan to release the blondies from the sides. Lift up on the foil handles to remove the blondies from the pan. Using a sharp knife, cut into 32 rectangles, about 1¼″ × 2½″ each. (The blondies will keep for up to 2 days, wrapped individually in plastic wrap and stored at room temperature.)

Makes 32 blondies

Chocolate Morsels: For a colorful variation, stir in 2 cups M&M's instead of chocolate chunks.

Lois's Brownies

During a brownie-baking demonstration at Williams-Sonoma's Manhattan store, I started a recipe-swapping chat with a very nice lady from Toronto named Lois. She suggested that I call for her famous brownie recipe, and I did. I discovered that she wasn't just any Lois but Lois Lilienstein of the enormously popular children's singing group, Sharon, Lois and Bram. It turns out she is as talented in the kitchen as she is onstage. Try her marshmallow-studded brownies—the marshmallows will melt and disappear into the batter, adding a chewy quality to these extrachocolaty delights.

12 tablespoons (1½ sticks) unsalted
   butter, cut into pieces
4 ounces unsweetened chocolate,
   chopped fine
1 cup granulated sugar
4 large eggs, at room temperature
1 teaspoon vanilla extract
1 cup all-purpose flour
¼ teaspoon baking powder
¼ teaspoon salt
2 cups loosely packed miniature
   marshmallows
4 ounces walnuts, toasted (see
   Index) and chopped coarse
   (about 1 cup)
1 6-ounce package (about 1 cup)
   semisweet chocolate chips

1. Position a rack in the center of the oven and preheat to 350°F. Line a 9″ × 13″ baking pan with a double thickness of aluminum foil so that the foil extends beyond the two opposite ends of the pan. Fold the overhang down to form handles. Lightly butter the bottom and sides of the foil-lined pan. Dust the inside of the pan with flour, tapping out excess.

2. In a medium saucepan over low heat, melt the butter. Off heat, add the unsweetened chocolate and let stand for 1 minute; whisk until smooth. Let stand until tepid, about 10 minutes. Whisk in the sugar. Whisk in the eggs, then the vanilla. Using a wooden spoon, stir in the flour, baking powder, and salt, just until smooth. Stir in the marshmallows, nuts, and chocolate chips.

3. Spread the batter into the prepared pan and bake for 25–30 minutes, until a toothpick inserted in the center comes out with a moist crumb. *Do not overbake.* Cool completely on a wire cake rack.

4. Run a knife around the inside edges of the pan to release the brownie from the sides. Lift up on the foil handles to remove the brownie from the pan. Using a sharp knife, cut into 12 pieces, about 2¼″ × 3¼″ each. (The brownies will keep for up to 3 days, individually wrapped in plastic wrap and stored at room temperature.)

Makes 12 brownies

Kiss Kookies

I've seen these chewy, peanutty cookies with a milk chocolate center under a variety of names—Peanut Butter Blossoms, Black-Eyed Susans, Buckeyes—but no matter what you call them, they are one of the best things you can put in a cookie jar.

1¾ cups all-purpose flour
1 teaspoon baking soda
½ teaspoon salt
8 tablespoons (1 stick) unsalted
    butter, softened
½ cup creamy peanut butter
1 cup granulated sugar, divided
½ cup packed light brown sugar
1 large egg, lightly beaten
2 tablespoons milk
1 teaspoon vanilla extract
36 Hershey's Milk Chocolate
    Kisses, unwrapped

1. Position a rack in the top third of the oven and preheat to 375°F. Sift together the flour, baking soda, and salt through a wire strainer onto a piece of wax paper.

2. In a large bowl, using a hand-held electric mixer set at high speed, beat the butter and peanut butter together until creamy, about 1 minute. Gradually add ½ cup of the granulated sugar and all the brown sugar and beat until light in color and consistency, about 2 minutes. Beat in the egg, milk, and vanilla. Using a wooden spoon, stir in the flour mixture.

3. Place the remaining ½ cup granulated sugar in a small bowl. Using a scant tablespoon of dough for each, form the dough into balls. Roll the balls in the sugar to coat them evenly, then place them about 1½ inches apart on ungreased baking sheets.

4. Bake, one sheet at a time, until the edges of the cookies are set, about 8 minutes. Remove the sheet from the oven and place a Hershey's Kiss in the center of each cookie. Return to the oven and continue baking until the cookies are lightly browned, about 2 minutes longer. Let the cookies cool on the sheet for 5 minutes, then transfer to wire cake racks to cool completely. Repeat the procedure with the remaining cookies. (The cookies can be prepared up to 2 days ahead and stored in an airtight container at room temperature, the layers separated with sheets of wax paper.)

Makes about 36 cookies

Texas Pecan and Chocolate Toffee Cookies

My culinary pen pal, Bobbie (she's my friend Mimi's mom), lives deep in the heart of Texas. Sometimes she sends me fresh, hard-to-find Mexican herbs from her garden. Other times she mails me yummy recipes like this one—crunchy, crusty, nutty squares iced with milk chocolate.

1 cup (2 sticks) unsalted butter,
    softened
1 cup packed light brown sugar
1 large egg yolk
1 teaspoon vanilla extract
1½ cups all-purpose flour
4 ounces pecans, toasted (see
    Index) and chopped fine (about
    1 cup)
1 6-ounce package (about 1 cup)
    milk chocolate or semisweet
    chocolate chips

1. Position a rack in the center of the oven and preheat to 350°F. Line a 9″ × 13″ baking pan with a double thickness of aluminum foil so that the foil extends beyond the two opposite ends of the pan. Fold the overhang down to form handles. Lightly butter the bottom and sides of the foil-lined pan.

2. In a large bowl, using a hand-held electric mixer set at high speed, beat the butter until creamy, about 1 minute. Add the brown sugar and beat until light in color and consistency, about 2 minutes. Beat in the egg yolk and vanilla. Using a wooden spoon, stir in the flour until smooth. Stir in the pecans. Press the dough firmly and evenly into the bottom of the foil-lined pan. Using a fork, pierce the dough all over.

3. Bake until the surface is lightly browned and the center feels set when pressed lightly with a finger, 20–25 minutes. Cool slightly in the pan on a wire cake rack, about 5 minutes.

4. Arrange the chocolate chips in a single layer over the surface of the slightly cooled cookies. Let stand until the chips are melted around the edges, about 5 minutes. Using a metal cake spatula, spread the milk chocolate evenly over the cookies. Using a sharp knife, cut the cookies while still warm into 32 pieces, about 1¾" × 2¼" each. Cool completely, until the chocolate is firm. Lift up on the foil handles to remove the cookies from the pan. (The cookies can be prepared up to 3 days ahead. Store the cookies in an airtight container at cool room temperature, separating the layers with sheets of wax paper.)

Makes 32 bar cookies

Cakey Chocolate Chip–Raisin Cookies

Here's an irresistible cookie with a soft, cakelike texture and the added goodness of raisins. If, like me, you are a cookie dunker, you'll find these puffy, light-textured treats really soak up the milk.

2 cups all-purpose flour
1 teaspoon baking powder
¾ teaspoon salt
½ teaspoon baking soda
8 tablespoons (1 stick) unsalted
   butter, softened
½ cup granulated sugar
¾ cup packed light brown sugar
1 large egg
1 large egg yolk
¾ teaspoon vanilla extract
1 6-ounce package (about 1 cup)
   semisweet chocolate chips
1 cup dark raisins

1. Position two racks in the center and top third of the oven and preheat to 350°F. Sift the flour, baking powder, salt, and baking soda together through a wire strainer onto a sheet of wax paper.

2. In a medium bowl, using a hand-held electric mixer set at high speed, beat the butter until creamy, about 1 minute. Still beating, add the granulated and brown sugars and continue beating until light in color and consistency, about 2 minutes. Beat in the egg and egg yolk and then the vanilla. Using a wooden spoon, stir in the flour mixture. Stir in the chocolate chips and raisins.

3. Drop the batter by rounded tablespoons, about 2 inches apart, onto ungreased baking sheets. Bake for 13–15 minutes, switching the baking sheets from the top rack to the center rack halfway through the baking, until the cookies are lightly browned around the edges. Let the cookies cool on the

sheets for 2 minutes. Transfer the cookies with a metal spatula to a wire cake rack and cool completely. (Store the cookies for up to 3 days in an airtight container at room temperature.)

Makes about 26 cookies

Chocolate Morsels: These cookies are meant to be tender and cakey, not gooey and chewy. Bake them completely through. It is an especially good idea to bake the first sheet alone as a test to get a handle on the baking time.

Try these with 2 cups of milk chocolate–covered raisins instead of the combined chips and raisins. I also like them with 1 cup chocolate-covered raisins and 1 cup chopped toasted walnuts.

Chewy Chocolate and
White Chocolate Chip Cookies

❧

*A chocolate chip cookie is not a chocolate chip cookie is not a chocolate chip cookie!
This cookie's chocolate-oats batter is chock-full of white chocolate chips, macadamia
nuts, and chopped dried apricots. Once baked, the chunky cookies are crispy around
the edges and gooey and chewy inside.*

1 ounce unsweetened chocolate,
   chopped fine
1 cup rolled oats (not instant)
¾ cup all-purpose flour
½ teaspoon baking soda
½ teaspoon salt
8 tablespoons (1 stick) unsalted
   butter, softened
½ cup granulated sugar
½ cup packed light brown sugar
1 large egg
1 teaspoon vanilla extract
½ cup white chocolate chips, such
   as Hershey's
½ cup coarsely chopped dried
   apricots
2 ounces macadamia nuts,
   chopped coarse and rinsed of
   salt (about ½ cup)

1. Position two racks in the top third and center of the oven and preheat
to 350°F. In the top part of a double boiler over hot, not simmering, water,
melt the chocolate, stirring often until smooth. Remove the top part of the
double boiler from the bottom and let the chocolate stand until tepid, about 10
minutes.

2. In a medium bowl, stir together the oats, flour, baking soda, and salt. In another medium bowl, using a hand-held electric mixer set at high speed, beat the butter until creamy, about 1 minute. Still beating, gradually add the granulated and brown sugars and beat until light in color and consistency, about 2 minutes. Beat in the egg, then the vanilla. Beat in the cooled chocolate. Using a wooden spoon, stir in the flour mixture. Stir in the chips, apricots, and macadamia nuts.

3. Drop the batter by rounded tablespoons, about 2 inches apart, onto ungreased baking sheets. Bake for 12–14 minutes, switching the baking sheets from the top rack to the center rack halfway through baking, until the cookies are lightly browned around the edges. Let the cookies cool on the sheets for 2 minutes. Transfer the cookies with a metal spatula to a wire cake rack and cool completely. (The cookies will keep for up to 5 days, stored in an airtight container at room temperature.)

Makes about 20 cookies

Chocolate Morsels: Please try to find white chocolate chips. While you can chop a 3-ounce bar of white chocolate into ¼-inch squares, I find that these "homemade chips" can sometimes scorch in the oven and get unpleasantly gritty.

Whenever I make cookies, I bake a single sheet first as a test batch to see how they set after cooling. All chocolate chip cookies are soft and gooey when they come out of the oven but can become hard and brittle when cooled if overbaked by even a minute or two. Adjust baking times according to your own preferences, using the lower number of minutes in the estimated baking times for moist, chewy cookies and the higher number for crisp, crunchy ones.

Diane's Triple-Layered Delights

A sweet treat from the recipe files of my cohort Diane Kniss. Diane's cookies have traveled around the world with her husband, Dick, who is the bassist for Peter, Paul and Mary. This recipe features a triple play of a chocolate pastry crust, a thin layer of melted chocolate, then a pecan pie–like topping. Intense, yes, but good!

CHOCOLATE CRUST LAYER
1 ounce semisweet chocolate
1¼ cups all-purpose flour
1 teaspoon baking powder
1 teaspoon granulated sugar
⅛ teaspoon salt
4 tablespoons (½ stick) unsalted
   butter, cut into pieces
1 large egg yolk
2 tablespoons cold strong brewed
   coffee

PECAN LAYER
½ cups granulated sugar
6 tablespoons (¾ stick) unsalted
   butter, softened
2 large eggs, at room temperature
2 teaspoons vanilla extract
8 ounces pecans, chopped coarse
   (about 2 cups)

2 6-ounce packages (about 2 cups)
   semisweet chocolate chips

1. *Make the crust:* Position a rack in the top third of the oven and preheat to 350°F. Lightly butter a 10½″ × 15½″ × 1″ jelly-roll pan.

2. In the top part of a double boiler over hot, not simmering, water, melt the chocolate, stirring often, until smooth. Remove the top part of the double boiler from the heat and let the chocolate cool until tepid, about 10 minutes.

3. In a food processor fitted with the metal blade, pulse the flour, baking powder, sugar, and salt. Add the butter and pulse until the mixture resembles coarse meal. Add the tepid chocolate, egg yolk, and coffee and pulse 10–15 times, just until the mixture is moistened. Gather up the dough and press evenly and firmly into the prepared pan.

4. Bake for 12–15 minutes, until the crust is set and lightly browned. Remove the pan from the oven and let cool for 2 minutes. Sprinkle the crust with the chocolate chips and let stand for 5 minutes, until the chips are softened. Using a metal cake spatula, spread the chips smoothly over the crust. Cool the crust on a wire cake rack until the chocolate layer is partially set, about 30 minutes.

5. *Make the pecan layer:* In a medium bowl, using a hand-held electric mixer set at high speed, cream the sugar and butter together until light in color and consistency, about 2 minutes. Add the eggs and vanilla and beat well. (The mixture may look curdled.) Stir in the pecans. Spoon the pecan mixture over the crust and spread it evenly with the spatula.

6. Return the pan to the oven and bake for 30 minutes, until the filling in the center of the pan looks opaque and is set. Cool completely on a wire cake rack. Using a sharp knife, cut into 36 bars, about $2\frac{1}{4}'' \times 2\frac{1}{2}''$ each. (The bars will keep for up to 3 days, stored in an airtight container at room temperature.)

Makes 36 bars

Chocolate Morsels: To keep the layers distinct, let the melted chocolate chip layer cool until it is partially set and tepid before spooning on the pecan layer.

Impossible Dream Bars

❧❧

How can something so easy be so good? These rich-as-sin bar cookies have a caramel taste reminiscent of a German chocolate cake. When you need a large batch of cookies in a hurry, turn to these for guaranteed success.

1½ cups graham cracker crumbs
12 tablespoons (1½ sticks) unsalted
   butter, melted
1 cup sweetened coconut flakes
1 6-ounce package (about 1 cup)
   semisweet chocolate chips
4 ounces walnuts, toasted (see
   Index) and chopped coarse
   (about 1 cup)
1 12-ounce can condensed milk

1. Position a rack in the center of the oven and preheat to 350°F. Line a 9″ × 13″ baking pan with a double thickness of aluminum foil so that the foil extends beyond the two opposite ends of the pan. Fold the overhang down to form handles. Lightly butter the bottom and sides of the foil-lined pan.

2. In a medium bowl, combine the graham cracker crumbs and melted butter. Press the mixture evenly into the bottom of the prepared pan. In this order, sprinkle the crumb layer with the coconut, chocolate chips, and walnuts. Drizzle the condensed milk evenly over the top of the layered mixture.

3. Bake until the condensed milk is golden brown and bubbling in the center of the pan, 25–30 minutes. Cool completely in the pan on a wire cake rack.

4. Run a sharp knife around the inside edges of the pan to release the bars from the sides. Lift up the foil handles to remove the cookies from the pan. Using a large sharp knife, cut into 24 bars, about 2¼″ × 2½″ each. The bars will keep for up to 3 days, stored in an airtight container at room temperature.

Makes about 24 bar cookies

Chocolate-Raisin Bread Pudding

Comfort food ne plus ultra. *This is one of my basic recipes, easy to alter at whim. Sometimes I add chopped apricots instead of the raisins, or toss in some chopped walnuts along with the fruit. You can serve it with sweetened whipped cream or vanilla ice cream. No matter what direction I take, it is always heaven on earth.*

1 loaf (about 9 ounces) Italian or
   French bread, cut into 1-inch
   squares
2 cups heavy (whipping) cream
1 cup milk
¾ cup granulated sugar
6 ounces semisweet chocolate,
   chopped fine
4 large eggs, at room temperature
1 teaspoon vanilla extract
1 cup dark raisins

1. Position a rack in the center of the oven and preheat to 350°F. Lightly butter a 9″ × 13″ baking pan. Place the bread cubes on a baking sheet and bake for 10 minutes, until slightly dried but not toasted.

2. In a medium saucepan, bring the cream, milk, and sugar to a low simmer over medium heat, stirring constantly to dissolve the sugar. Remove from the heat and add the chocolate. Let stand for 5 minutes, until the chocolate is softened, then whisk until smooth.

3. In a large bowl, whisk the eggs and vanilla until combined. Gradually beat in the hot milk mixture. Add the bread cubes and raisins and let stand for 10 minutes, stirring often. Transfer the mixture to the prepared pan.

4. Bake until the custard is set in the center, about 45 minutes. Let the pudding stand for 10 minutes before serving it hot, warm, or at room temperature.

Makes 6–8 servings

Chocolate Peanut Pie

Chocolate and peanuts are mated in an exceptional chocolate version of pecan pie. I like to serve this with sweetened whipped cream, sometimes spiked with a dash of bourbon.

PASTRY
1½ cups all-purpose flour
½ teaspoon salt
⅓ cup vegetable shortening, chilled and cut into pieces
2 tablespoons unsalted butter, chilled and cut into pieces
About ¼ cup ice water

FILLING
4 ounces semisweet chocolate, chopped fine
3 large eggs
1 cup light corn syrup
⅓ cup granulated sugar
2 tablespoons unsalted butter, melted
1 teaspoon vanilla extract
6 ounces (about 1½ cups) peanut halves

1. *Make the pastry:* In a medium bowl, stir together the flour and salt. Using a pastry blender or two knives, cut in the shortening and butter until the mixture resembles coarse meal. Tossing with a fork, gradually sprinkle in the ice water, mixing just until the dough is moist enough to hold together when pinched between the thumb and forefinger. (You may need to add more ice water.) Gather the dough into a thick disk, wrap it in wax paper, and chill for at least 1 hour or overnight.

2. On a lightly floured work surface, roll out the pastry into an 11- to 12-inch circle about ⅛ inch thick. (If the dough cracks, it is too cold. Let stand at room temperature for 5 minutes before proceeding.) Ease the dough into a 9-inch pie plate. Roll the excess dough over to form a rope, then crimp the dough decoratively. Place the pie plate on a baking sheet.

3. *Make the filling:* Position a rack in the center of the oven and preheat to 350°F. In the top part of a double boiler over hot, not simmering, water, melt the chocolate, stirring occasionally, until smooth. Remove the top part of

the double boiler from the bottom and let the chocolate cool until tepid, about 10 minutes.

4. In a medium bowl, whisk the eggs well. Add the cooled chocolate, corn syrup, sugar, melted butter, and vanilla and whisk well. Stir in the peanuts. Pour the mixture into the prepared pie shell.

5. Bake until a knife inserted halfway between the center and the edge of the pie comes out clean, 50-60 minutes. Cool the pie completely on a wire cake rack. (The pie can be prepared up to 2 days ahead, covered with plastic wrap, and stored at room temperature.)

Makes 6–8 servings

Mississippi Mud Cake

The biggest, gooiest brownie you've ever taken a spoon to, my version of this new American classic includes a good splash of bourbon and a handful of pecans to lend it that south-of-the-Mason-Dixon-line flair. (If you're sharing this cake with youngsters, substitute strong brewed coffee for the bourbon. The cake will not have a strong coffee flavor.) I usually serve this simply, with whipped cream, but if you are in the mood to overindulge, top each portion with your favorite hot fudge sauce and the South will rise again!

1½ cups (3 sticks) unsalted butter,
    cut into pieces
6 ounces unsweetened chocolate,
    chopped fine
1½ cups granulated sugar
2 tablespoons light corn syrup
5 large eggs, at room temperature
6 tablespoons bourbon, divided
1½ teaspoons vanilla extract,
    divided
1 cup all-purpose flour
3 ounces pecans, chopped fine
    (about ¾ cup)
¼ teaspoon salt
1 cup heavy (whipping) cream
2 tablespoons confectioners' sugar

1. Position a rack in the center of the oven and preheat to 350°F. Lightly butter and then flour a 9-inch round springform pan, tapping out excess flour.

2. In a large saucepan over medium heat, melt the butter. Remove the pan from the heat, add the chocolate, and let stand until the chocolate is softened, about 3 minutes. Whisk until smooth and let stand until tepid, about 10 minutes. Whisk in the sugar and corn syrup. One at a time, whisk in the

eggs. Add 3 tablespoons of the bourbon and 1 teaspoon of the vanilla and whisk well. Using a wooden spoon, stir in the flour, pecans, and salt. Scrape the batter into the prepared pan and smooth the top evenly with a rubber spatula.

3. Bake until a toothpick inserted in the center comes out with a moist crumb, about 45 minutes. (Do not overbake. The center of the cake should remain moist.) Remove the cake from the oven and sprinkle with the remaining 3 tablespoons bourbon. Cool the cake completely in the pan on a wire cake rack.

4. Run a sharp knife around the edges of the cake to loosen it, then release and remove the sides of the springform pan. Wrap the cake tightly in plastic wrap and refrigerate for at least 4 hours or overnight. Remove the cake from the refrigerator 1 hour before serving. (The cake can be prepared up to 2 days ahead, wrapped in plastic wrap, and refrigerated.)

5. In a chilled medium bowl, using a hand-held electric mixer set at high speed, beat the cream, confectioners' sugar, and remaining ½ teaspoon vanilla until soft peaks begin to form. Serve the cake garnished with a dollop of whipped cream.

Makes 8–10 servings

Chocolate Swirl Cheesecake with Chocolate-Nut Crust

꙳

This cheesecake has a heavenly texture, made supercreamy with lots and lots of sour cream. The crust, a seductive blend of chocolate wafer crumbs, hazelnuts, and spices, adds another fillip. To be sure the delicate cheesecake sets properly, chill at least overnight.

CRUST

4 ounces hazelnuts, toasted and skinned (about 1 cup; see Index)
⅔ cup (about 3 ounces) crushed chocolate wafer cookies
¼ teaspoon ground cinnamon
¼ teaspoon freshly grated nutmeg

FILLING

1 pound cream cheese, softened
1 cup granulated sugar
3 cups sour cream
3 large eggs
1 teaspoon vanilla extract
2 ounces semisweet chocolate, chopped fine
1 teaspoon vegetable oil

1. *Make the crust:* Position a rack in the center of the oven and preheat to 325°F. Lightly butter the bottom and sides of a 9-inch round springform pan.

2. In a food processor fitted with the metal blade, process the hazelnuts until very finely chopped and slightly oily. Add the cookie crumbs, cinnamon, and nutmeg and process until well combined. Press the mixture evenly and firmly into the bottom and 1 inch up the sides of the prepared pan. Refrigerate the crust while making the filling.

3. *Make the filling:* In a large bowl, using a hand-held electric mixer set at high speed, beat the cream cheese until smooth. Gradually add the sugar and beat well. Beat in the sour cream. One at a time, beat in the eggs and then the vanilla, scraping the sides of the bowl well with a rubber spatula. Scrape the filling into the crust-lined pan, smoothing the top evenly with the spatula.

4. In the top part of a double boiler over hot, not simmering, water, melt the chocolate and vegetable oil together, stirring often, until smooth.

Remove the top part of the double boiler from the bottom and let the mixture cool until tepid, about 10 minutes. Drizzle the chocolate mixture over the surface of the cheesecake in a random swirling pattern. Using a knife, cut through the drizzles, moving the knife back and forth to create a feathered effect.

5. Bake for about 1½ hours, until the cheesecake has risen and the edges are beginning to brown slightly. Run a thin, sharp knife around the inside edges of the cheesecake to loosen it from the sides of the pan. Cool the cheesecake completely on a wire cake rack. When cool, cover with plastic wrap and refrigerate for at least 8 hours or overnight.

6. Release the sides of the springform pan and slice, using a thin, sharp knife dipped in hot water and wiped dry between cuts. (The cheesecake can be prepared up to 3 days ahead, covered with plastic wrap, and refrigerated.)

Makes 10–12 servings

Chocolate Cranberry Cheesecake

Chocolate Cranberry Cheesecake is as much a holiday tradition on my dinner table as pumpkin pie. The cranberries' citrus tang is beautifully complemented by the winelike undertones found in fine bittersweet chocolate. While I can almost guarantee that everyone will ask for seconds, start by serving your guests thin slices, please . . . this is a killer dessert.

CHOCOLATE WAFER CRUST
1⅓ cups (about 6 ounces) crushed
    chocolate wafer cookies
¼ cup granulated sugar
4 tablespoons (½ stick) unsalted
    butter, melted

FILLING
2 cups fresh or frozen cranberries
2 cups water
¾ cup granulated sugar, divided
2 8-ounce packages cream cheese,
    at room temperature
2 large eggs, at room temperature
¾ cup sour cream
1 tablespoon cornstarch

GLAZE
¾ cup heavy (whipping) cream
8 ounces bittersweet chocolate,
    chopped fine

Chocolate curls for garnish (see
    Index)

1. *Make the crust:* Position a rack in the center of the oven and preheat to 350°F. Lightly butter the bottom and sides of a 9-inch springform pan. In a medium bowl, mix together the cookie crumbs, sugar, and melted butter until combined. Press the cookie mixture evenly onto the bottom and 1 inch up the sides of the prepared pan. Set aside.

2. *Make the filling:* In a medium saucepan, combine the cranberries, water, and ¼ cup of the sugar. Bring to a boil over medium-high heat, stirring often to dissolve the sugar. Reduce the heat to low and simmer, stirring often to prevent scorching, until the mixture is reduced to about 1 cup, 8–10 minutes. Transfer the mixture to a medium bowl and cool completely, stirring often.

74

3. In a large bowl, using a hand-held electric mixer set at medium-high speed, beat the cream cheese until smooth, about 1 minute. Add the remaining ½ cup sugar and beat until well combined, about 1 minute. One at a time, beat in the eggs. Add ½ cup of the cranberry mixture, the sour cream, and the cornstarch. Mix until blended, scraping the sides of the bowl often with a rubber spatula. Pour the mixture into the prepared pan and dot the surface with heaped teaspoons of the remaining cranberry mixture.

4. Bake the cheesecake for 15 minutes. Reduce the heat to 325°F and continue baking until the edges have risen and begun to brown, about 35 minutes longer. Run a thin, sharp knife around the inside edges of the cheesecake to loosen the cheesecake from the sides of the pan. Cool the cheesecake completely on a wire cake rack. When cool, release the sides of the springform pan and wrap the cheesecake, still on the bottom of the pan, in plastic wrap. Refrigerate until well chilled, at least 4 hours or overnight.

5. *Make the glaze:* In a medium saucepan, bring the cream just to a low simmer over medium heat. Remove the pan from the heat, add the chocolate, and let stand until melted, about 1 minute, then whisk until smooth. Transfer to a medium bowl and let stand until tepid but still pourable, about 20 minutes.

6. Unwrap the chilled cheesecake and place it on a wire cake rack set over a wax paper–lined work surface. Pour the cooled glaze onto the middle of the cheesecake. Using a metal cake spatula, spread the glaze evenly over the top of the cheesecake, letting the excess run down the sides. Smooth the sides of the cheesecake, scooping up excess glaze from the wax paper to cover any bare spots if necessary. Transfer the cheesecake to a serving dish and refrigerate until the glaze is set, about 30 minutes. (The cheesecake can be prepared up to 1 day ahead and covered loosely with plastic wrap after the glaze has set. The glaze will lose its sheen, but it will return if the cheesecake is allowed to stand at room temperature for about 1 hour before being served.) Just before serving, garnish with the chocolate curls.

Makes 10–14 servings

7
A Taste of Europe

Sachertorte
Marjolaine Classique
Chocolate Raspberry Trifle
Chocolate Terrine with Chocolate and Strawberry Drizzles
Grand Marnier Truffles
Passionate White Chocolate Truffles
Swiss Truffle Loaf
Rigo Jansci
Chocolate Bûche de Noël
Grand Indulgence Hot Chocolate
Tropical Chocolate Fondue with Seasonal Fruits
Chocolate French Toast
White Chocolate Coeur à la Crème
Chocolate-Dipped Orange Cookies
Tiramisù
Spuma di Caffé Latte

Sachertorte

❦

Mecca or Rome may be the destination for religious pilgrimages, but for the chocolate aficionado it is Vienna. Every little twist in the cobblestoned streets reveals another mouthwatering konditeri *(a combination bakeshop/candy store/coffee shop). It's interesting to note that while there are about 20 so-called "authentic" Sachertorte recipes, all supposedly direct from the Hotel Sacher's pastry kitchens, each is different. Mine is an unauthorized version but tastes just as scrumptious. You'll be equally enraptured by this dense, nutty chocolate cake, accented with a veneer of apricot preserves, then cloaked in a shiny glaze, with the word* Sacher *emblazoned across the top.*

CAKE

12 tablespoons (1½ sticks) unsalted
   butter, cut into pieces
6 ounces bittersweet chocolate,
   chopped fine
2 ounces sliced blanched almonds
   (about ½ cup)
1 cup granulated sugar, divided
5 large eggs, separated, at room
   temperature
1 teaspoon vanilla extract
1 cup all-purpose flour
¼ teaspoon salt
⅓ cup apricot preserves

GLAZE

½ cup heavy (whipping) cream
5 ounces bittersweet chocolate,
   chopped fine
2 tablespoons unsalted butter, cut
   into pieces
1 tablespoon light corn syrup

1. *Make the cake:* Position a rack in the center of the oven and preheat to 350°F. Lightly butter and then flour the inside of a 9-inch round springform pan, tapping out excess flour.

2. In a medium saucepan over low heat, melt the butter. Remove the pan from the heat, add the chocolate, and let stand until melted, about 3 minutes; whisk until smooth. Let the chocolate stand until tepid, about 10 minutes.

3. In a food processor fitted with the metal blade, combine the almonds with ¼ cup of the sugar. Pulse the mixture 15–20 times, or until as finely chopped as possible. Set the almond mixture aside.

4. Using a rubber spatula, transfer the chocolate mixture to a medium bowl. Whisk in the remaining ¾ cup sugar, the egg yolks, then the vanilla. Add the flour, almond mixture, and salt; whisk until smooth.

5. In a medium-size grease-free bowl, using a hand-held electric mixer set at low speed, with clean, dry beaters, beat the egg whites until foamy. Increase the speed to high and beat just until stiff peaks begin to form. Stir about one-fourth of the beaten whites into the chocolate mixture to lighten it. Using a rubber spatula, gently fold in the remaining whites. Spread the batter into the prepared pan and smooth the top.

6. Bake until a toothpick inserted in the center of the cake comes out with a moist crumb, 35–40 minutes. Cool the cake on a wire cake rack for 10 minutes. Run a sharp knife around the inside edges of the pan to loosen the cake from the sides. Remove the sides of the springform pan and cool the cake completely on the rack.

7. In a small saucepan, heat the preserves over low heat, stirring often with a wooden spoon, until they come to a boil. Strain and rub the preserves through a wire strainer into a small bowl.

8. Using a metal cake spatula, spread the apricot preserves evenly over the top of the cake. Let the apricot preserves cool until set, about 15 minutes.

9. *Make the glaze:* In a small saucepan over medium heat, bring the cream to a low simmer. Off the heat, add the chocolate, butter, and corn syrup. Let the mixture stand until the chocolate is melted, about 3 minutes, then whisk until smooth. Let the glaze stand until tepid and slightly thickened, about 20 minutes. Transfer ¼ cup of the glaze to a small plastic sandwich bag and set aside.

10. Place the cake on the wire cake rack on a wax paper–lined work surface. Pour the glaze over the top of the cake. Using a metal cake spatula, smooth the glaze over the top of the cake, letting the excess run down the sides. Use the spatula to pick up any excess glaze on the wax paper and cover any bare spots. Let the cake stand until the glaze is partially set, about 20 minutes.

11. Squeeze the glaze in the plastic bag into one corner of the bag. Twist the bag closed to form a small pastry bag. Using scissors, snip a $\frac{1}{4}$-inch opening off the glaze-filled corner of the bag. Squeezing the glaze out of the bag, write the word *Sacher* across the surface of the cake. The glaze should be cooled and thick enough to write with easily. If the glaze is too thick to flow, reheat slightly in a microwave oven until it reaches the proper consistency. Refrigerate the cake, uncovered, until the glaze is firm, about 1 hour. Remove the cake from the refrigerator 1 hour before serving. (The cake can be prepared up to 1 day ahead, covered loosely with plastic wrap, and refrigerated.)

Makes 8–10 servings

Marjolaine Classique

Le Pyramide, a bastion of French haute cuisine before Julia Child was knee-high to a whisk, made marjolaine famous. It is a superlative dessert of nut meringues, called dacquoise, *layered with three heavenly fillings: vanilla cream, espresso-mocha, and orange liqueur. My recipe is inspired by a version by David Leiderman and Michelle Utvater in* Cooking the Nouvelle Cuisine in America.

DACQUOISE LAYERS

6 ounces (1½ cups) whole blanched almonds, toasted (see Index)
6 ounces (1½ cups) hazelnuts, toasted and peeled (see Index)
1¼ cups granulated sugar, divided
2 tablespoons all-purpose flour
8 large egg whites, at room temperature
¼ teaspoon salt

FILLINGS

1 quart heavy (whipping) cream, divided
1 pound bittersweet chocolate, chopped fine
1 teaspoon instant espresso powder
1 tablespoon boiling water
½ cup superfine sugar
8 tablespoons (1 stick) unsalted butter
1 teaspoon vanilla extract
Grated zest of 1 small orange
2 tablespoons Grand Marnier, or other orange-flavored liqueur

1. *Make the dacquoise:* Position a rack in the center of the oven and preheat to 325°F. Lightly butter the inside of a 17″ × 11″ jelly-roll pan. Line the bottom and sides of the pan with parchment paper. To do so, cut off a 19″ × 13″ piece of parchment paper. Using scissors, cut four diagonal slashes, each about 3 inches long, in from each of the four corners of the paper. Fit the parchment paper into the pan to line the bottom and sides, folding over the corners at the slashes.

2. In a food processor fitted with the metal blade, pulse the toasted almonds and hazelnuts with ½ cup of the sugar until very finely chopped but not oily. Add the remaining ¾ cup sugar and the flour and pulse until combined.

3. In a large grease-free bowl, using a hand-held electric mixer set at low speed, with clean, dry beaters, beat the egg whites until foamy. Add the salt, increase the speed to high, and beat just until the whites form stiff peaks. Using a large rubber spatula, fold the nut mixture into the beaten whites. Using a cake spatula, preferably metal, spread the meringue evenly into the prepared pan, being sure to reach the corners.

4. Bake until the dacquoise is lightly browned but still pliable, about 35 minutes. Invert it onto a large wire cake rack or a clean kitchen towel. Peel off the parchment paper. Using a serrated knife, cut the dacquoise vertically into four 4¼″ × 11″ strips. Cool completely. (The dacquoise strips can be prepared up to 1 day ahead, wrapped individually in aluminum foil, and stored at room temperature.)

5. *Make the fillings:* In a medium saucepan over medium heat, bring 2 cups of the heavy cream to a low simmer. Remove the pan from the heat, add the chocolate, and let stand for 1 minute. Whisk until melted and smooth.

6. Pour about one-third of the chocolate mixture (approximately 1¼ cups) into a medium bowl. In a small bowl, dissolve the espresso powder in the boiling water. Stir this into the chocolate mixture in the bowl. Let both the chocolate and espresso-mocha mixtures cool at room temperature until thickened to a puddinglike consistency, at least 2 hours. (The chocolate fillings can be prepared up to 1 day ahead and stored at room temperature. Do not refrigerate, or they will become too firm.)

7. In a medium saucepan, cook the superfine sugar and butter over medium-low heat, stirring constantly, until the sugar begins to melt into the butter, about 2 minutes. Remove from the heat and cool completely.

8. In a large chilled bowl, using a hand-held electric mixer set at high speed, whip the remaining 2 cups heavy cream just until stiff peaks form. Transfer half of the whipped cream to a medium bowl. Whisk half of the butter mixture into each bowl of whipped cream. Whisk the vanilla into one bowl. Whisk the orange zest and Grand Marnier into the other bowl. Refrigerate the vanilla and Grand Marnier fillings until firm enough to spread, about 30 minutes.

9. *Assemble the marjolaine:* Place three dacquoise layers on a work surface. Spread one with the vanilla cream. Spread another with the espresso-

mocha mixture. Spread the third with the Grand Marnier filling. (If the fillings seem soft, place the layers on baking sheets and refrigerate until firm.) Stack the layers on a large serving platter—vanilla on the bottom, then espresso-mocha, and then Grand Marnier. Top with the plain dacquoise layer. Using a metal cake spatula, smooth any excess filling that oozes from the sides. (Don't worry about keeping the fillings distinct; they will be covered in frosting later.) Cover the marjolaine loosely with plastic wrap and refrigerate for 30 minutes.

10. Using a metal cake spatula, frost the top and sides of the cake with the chocolate mixture. (Don't frost the short ends.) Refrigerate until the frosting is set, about 30 minutes. Loosely wrap the marjolaine in plastic wrap, pressing the wrap directly onto the open surfaces of the short ends, and refrigerate for at least 4 hours or overnight. (The marjolaine can be prepared up to 2 days ahead. As the marjolaine stands, the crunchy texture of the nut layers will soften.) Using a serrated knife, cut the marjolaine into ¾-inch slices.

Makes 10–12 servings

Chocolate Raspberry Trifle

An awe-inspiring, enormous masterpiece of sweetness, a British trifle is anything but a middling affair. It is one of my favorite desserts for feeding a crowd—I've found it is impossible to make trifle for fewer than eight guests. You may substitute ¾ cup orange juice for the sherry and brandy. Remember that the cake for the trifle should be made at least 24 hours ahead of time, and then the assembled dessert must chill— so plan ahead.

Chocolate Pound Cake (see Index)
2 cups half-and-half
½ cup granulated sugar
6 large egg yolks, at room
    temperature
2 teaspoons vanilla extract
1 cup seedless raspberry jam
½ cup medium-dry sherry, such as
    Oloroso
¼ cup brandy
2 pints fresh or defrosted frozen
    raspberries
1 cup heavy (whipping) cream
2 tablespoons confectioners' sugar
Fresh raspberries for garnish

1. At least 1 day before making the trifle, make the Chocolate Pound Cake.

2. In a heavy-bottomed medium saucepan, bring the half-and-half and sugar to a simmer over medium-low heat, stirring often to dissolve the sugar. In a small bowl, whisk the egg yolks until lightly beaten. Gradually whisk about one-fourth of the hot half-and-half mixture into the yolks. Pour the egg mixture back into the saucepan and cook over low heat, stirring constantly with a wooden spoon, until the custard has thickened enough to coat the back of the spoon, 3–4 minutes. (An instant-read thermometer inserted in the custard will

84

read about 175°F.) Do not let the custard boil. Strain the mixture through a wire strainer into a medium bowl. Stir in the vanilla. Let the custard cool completely.

3. Cut the Chocolate Pound Cake into ¾-inch-thick slices. Line the inside of a large glass bowl (about 3-quart capacity) with some of the cake slices. (They don't have to be a perfect fit.) Using the back of a spoon, spread the cake slices with the raspberry jam. Cut the remaining slices into 1-inch cubes.

4. In a glass measuring cup, combine the sherry and brandy. Sprinkle ½ cup of the sherry mixture over the arranged cake slices. Place 1 pint of the raspberries in the bowl and top with the cake cubes. Sprinkle the remaining ¼ cup sherry mixture over the cubes. Sprinkle the remaining pint of raspberries over the cake cubes. Pour the cooled custard over all.

5. In a large chilled bowl, using a hand-held electric mixer set at high speed, whip the heavy cream just until soft peaks form. Beat in the confectioners' sugar. Transfer the whipped cream to a pastry bag fitted with a large star tip such as Ateco #5. Pipe swirls of whipped cream over the top of the trifle and garnish with fresh raspberries. Cover with plastic wrap and refrigerate for at least 2 hours or overnight.

Makes 8 servings

Chocolate Morsels: Because slightly stale cake seems to soak up the liquids better than fresh cake does, making the cake 1 day ahead of time is suggested. Frankly, I've enjoyed the trifle with cakes both stale and fresh.

Chocolate Terrine with
Chocolate and Strawberry Drizzles

I often spend summer vacation in Paris studying the latest trends in pastry arts. Many Parisian restaurants offer marquise au chocolat, *a chocolate mousse so dense and fudgy it can be sliced like a pâté. The chocolate and strawberry drizzles are a lot of fun, and you'll be able to express all those pent-up modern artist tendencies. So, the next time you want to turn your dining room into a French bistro, voilà, this is the dessert for you!*

TERRINE
9 ounces bittersweet chocolate, chopped fine
½ cup confectioners' sugar
12 tablespoons (1½ sticks) unsalted butter, softened and cut into 12 pieces.
5 large eggs, separated, at room temperature
Grated zest of 1 large orange
2 tablespoons Grand Marnier or other orange-flavored liqueur
Pinch of salt

SAUCE
2 10-ounce packages frozen strawberries in light syrup, defrosted and drained
2 tablespoons superfine sugar or to taste

CHOCOLATE SYRUP
½ cup heavy (whipping) cream
1 tablespoon light corn syrup
4 ounces bittersweet chocolate, chopped fine
Fresh strawberries for garnish (optional)

1. *Make the terrine:* In a heatproof large bowl fitted over the top of a medium saucepan of hot, not simmering, water, melt the chocolate, stirring occasionally until smooth. Remove the bowl from the saucepan. Whisk in the confectioners' sugar. One piece at a time, whisk in the butter. Whisk in the egg yolks, orange zest, and Grand Marnier.

2. In a medium-size grease-free bowl, using a hand-held electric mixer set at medium-low speed, with clean, dry beaters, beat the egg whites until foamy. Add the salt, increase the speed to medium-high, and beat until soft

peaks begin to form. Stir about one-fourth of the beaten egg whites into the chocolate mixture to lighten it. Using a rubber spatula, fold in the remaining whites.

3. Rinse an 8″ × 4″ loaf pan with cold water. Line the bottom of the pan with wax paper or parchment paper. Transfer the chocolate mixture to the prepared pan, cover with plastic wrap, and refrigerate until firm, at least 4 hours or overnight.

4. *Make the strawberry sauce:* In a food processor fitted with the metal blade or a blender, puree the strawberries and superfine sugar together. Transfer the puree to a plastic squeeze container with a small tip, such as a ketchup container.

5. *Make the chocolate syrup:* In a small saucepan, bring the cream and corn syrup to a simmer over medium-low heat. Remove the saucepan from the heat, add the chocolate, and let stand for 2 minutes. Whisk until smooth. Transfer the chocolate mixture to a small bowl and cool completely. Do not refrigerate, or it will harden. Transfer the cooled chocolate syrup to another plastic squeeze container.

6. *Assemble the terrine:* Run a thin, sharp knife around the edges of the terrine to release it from the sides. Invert the terrine onto a platter and remove the wax paper. Using a thin, sharp knife dipped into hot water and dried between slicings, slice the terrine into ¾- to 1-inch-thick slices.

7. Using the strawberry sauce and chocolate syrup, squeeze abstract drizzle designs onto each serving plate. Using a spatula, transfer a slice of terrine onto each plate, garnish with fresh strawberries, and serve immediately. (The terrine and strawberry sauce can be prepared up to 1 day ahead, covered, and refrigerated. The chocolate sauce can also be prepared up to 1 day ahead, but store it at room temperature.)

Makes 8–10 servings

Grand Marnier Truffles

When I catered early-evening soirees at the French Embassy, I served Grand Marnier Truffles about half an hour before the end of the party. This subtle change from savory appetizers to sweet chocolate was a sophisticated signal that the evening was about to wind down. (At least it was classier than blinking the lights on and off.) At holiday time I turn my kitchen into a truffle factory—and if the truffles don't show up under the Christmas tree as gifts, I hear about it from my friends!

12 tablespoons (1½ sticks) unsalted
 butter, cut into pieces
1 pound bittersweet chocolate,
 chopped fine
½ cup orange marmalade,
 preferably bitter orange
¼ cup Grand Marnier or other
 orange-flavored liqueur
½ cup Dutch-process cocoa
 powder, such as Droste

1. In the top part of a double boiler over hot, not simmering, water, melt the butter. Add the chocolate and melt, stirring occasionally, until smooth. Remove the top part of the double boiler from the bottom.

2. Add the orange marmalade and Grand Marnier and whisk until smooth. Cover with plastic wrap and refrigerate until firm, about 4 hours or overnight. Or freeze the mixture until firm, about 2 hours.

3. Place the cocoa powder in a shallow medium bowl. Using a melon baller or a teaspoon, scoop about 1 tablespoon of the chilled chocolate mixture and roll between your palms to form a round truffle. Roll the truffle in the cocoa and transfer it to a baking sheet. Repeat the procedure with the remaining chocolate mixture. Cover the truffles tightly with plastic wrap and refrigerate until ready to serve. Remove them from the refrigerator 10 minutes before serving. (The truffles can be prepared up to 5 days ahead, stored in

tightly closed plastic bags, and refrigerated. They can be frozen for up to 1 month, wrapped tightly in double plastic bags.)

Makes about 35 truffles

Chocolate Morsels: Other fruit preserves and liquors can be substituted for the orange marmalade and Grand Marnier. Try strawberry preserves and cognac, apricot preserves and rum, strained raspberry preserves (not seedless) and Chambord, or cherry preserves and kirsch. Use only fruit preserves—jams and jellies are too sweet.

Passionate White Chocolate Truffles

There's nothing quite like the exotic combination of white chocolate and passion fruit. I recommend searching out the passion fruit liqueur for a true taste of the tropics; however, dark rum makes an acceptable, but differently flavored, substitute.

¼ cup (about 1 ounce) finely
    chopped dried papaya
¼ cup passion fruit liqueur, such
    as La Grande Passion
4 tablespoons (½ stick) unsalted
    butter, cut into pieces
8 ounces high-quality imported
    white chocolate, chopped fine
1 large egg yolk
2 ounces macadamia nuts, rinsed
    of salt, patted dry, and chopped
    fine (about ½ cup)

1. Place the papaya in a fine-meshed sieve and rinse under hot running water to remove any excess coloring. In a small bowl, combine the rinsed papaya with the passion fruit liqueur. Let stand for at least 1 hour or overnight.

2. In the top part of a double boiler set over hot, not simmering, water, melt the butter. Add about one-half of the white chocolate and melt, stirring occasionally, until almost smooth. Add the remaining white chocolate and melt, stirring occasionally, until smooth. Do not overstir the chocolate. Remove the top part of the double boiler from the water.

3. Whisk in the egg yolk and papaya-liqueur mixture. If the mixture separates, keep whisking until it comes together. Cover with plastic wrap and refrigerate until firm, about 4 hours or overnight.

4. Place the chopped nuts in a medium bowl. Using a melon baller or a teaspoon, scoop about 1 tablespoon of the chilled white chocolate mixture and roll it between your palms to form a round truffle. Roll the truffle in the nuts,

pressing them to adhere, and lay it on a wax paper–lined baking sheet. Repeat the procedure with the remaining chocolate mixture.

5. Cover the truffles tightly with plastic wrap and refrigerate until ready to serve. Remove them from the refrigerator 10 minutes before serving. (The truffles can be prepared up to 5 days ahead, stored in tightly closed plastic bags, and refrigerated. They can be frozen for up to 1 month, wrapped tightly in double plastic bags.)

Makes about 24 truffles

Chocolate Morsels: To make Pineapple-Rum Truffles, substitute dried pineapple for the papaya and dark rum for the passion fruit liqueur.

Swiss Truffle Loaf

A few summers ago I finally had my dream vacation: working at the Carma chocolate factory near Zurich, Switzerland. Nearly every Swiss bakery serves its own version of this uniquely pentagonal loaf cake filled with a creamy chocolate truffle mixture. Here's my rendition, sure to inspire yodels of appreciation from your lucky guests.

GENOISE
¾ cup plus 1 tablespoon sifted
    cake flour
¼ cup plus 1 tablespoon sifted
    nonalkalized cocoa powder, such
    as Hershey's
½ cup plus 1 tablespoon
    granulated sugar, divided
⅛ teaspoon baking soda
⅛ teaspoon salt
6 tablespoons (¾ stick) unsalted
    butter
3 large eggs
2 large egg yolks
1 teaspoon vanilla extract

GANACHE
1 cup heavy (whipping) cream
10 ounces bittersweet chocolate,
    chopped fine
2 tablespoons kirsch

SUGAR SYRUP
⅓ cup water
¼ cup granulated sugar
3 tablespoons kirsch

¼ cup Dutch-process cocoa
    powder, such as Droste, for
    garnish

1. *Make the genoise:* Position a rack in the center of the oven and preheat to 325°F. Lightly butter the inside of an 8″ × 4″ loaf pan. Line the bottom of the pan with a rectangle of wax paper. Dust the sides of the pan with flour and tap out excess. Sift the flour, cocoa, 1 tablespoon of the sugar, the baking soda and the salt together onto a piece of wax paper.

2. In a small saucepan, melt the butter and bring it to a boil over low heat. Pour the melted butter into a glass measuring cup and let stand for 5 minutes. Skim off any foam that is floating on the surface of the melted butter. Slowly pour off the clear yellow melted butter into a small bowl, discarding the milky white solids that have sunk to the bottom of the measuring cup. Set the bowl of melted butter aside.

3. In a large heatproof bowl, whisk the eggs and yolks until blended. Whisk in the remaining ½ cup sugar. Set the bowl over a medium saucepan of hot, not simmering, water. (The bottom of the bowl must touch the water.) Whisk constantly until the sugar is dissolved and the mixture is hot to the touch (110–120°F), about 3 minutes. Remove the bowl from the hot water.

4. Using a hand-held electric mixer set at high speed, beat the hot egg mixture until it is pale yellow and has tripled in volume, about 5 minutes. Beat in the vanilla.

5. Resift about one-third of the flour mixture over the batter. Using a large balloon whisk, fold in the flour mixture. In two more additions, resift and fold in the remaining flour mixture. (Don't worry if some flour remains visible.)

6. Spoon about one-fourth of the batter into the reserved melted butter and whisk until smooth. Pour the butter mixture into the batter and fold together with the whisk just until combined. Scrape the batter into the prepared pan and spread it evenly with a rubber spatula.

7. Bake until the top of the cake springs back when pressed lightly with a finger, 40–50 minutes. Cool the cake on a wire cake rack for 10 minutes. Run a thin, sharp knife around the edge of the cake to loosen it from the pan. Invert the cake onto a wire cake rack and peel off the wax paper. Carefully turn the cake so it is standing right side up; cool completely. Wrap the cake tightly in plastic wrap. (The cake can be prepared up to 1 day ahead and stored at room temperature.)

8. *Make the ganache:* In a small saucepan set over medium heat, bring the cream to a low simmer. Remove the pan from the heat and add the chocolate. Let stand for 1 minute, then whisk until smooth. Whisk in the kirsch. Transfer 1 cup of the ganache to a heatproof medium bowl and cover with plastic wrap. Refrigerate this portion of the ganache until it has thickened to puddinglike consistency, about 40 minutes. Let the remaining ganache stand at room temperature.

9. *Make the sugar syrup:* In a small saucepan, combine the water and sugar. Cook over medium-low heat, stirring constantly with a wooden spoon, just until the sugar dissolves. Raise the heat to medium-high and bring the syrup to a full boil. Transfer the syrup to a small bowl and cool completely. Stir in the kirsch.

10. *Assemble the cake:* Unwrap the genoise. Using a long, sharp knife, trim the dry edges from the sides and ends of the cake. Trim the top of the cake so that it is completely level. Using a small, sharp knife, trace a V on both short sides of the cake. The two Vs should start in the two top corners of each short end of the cake, and the points should meet in the middle of the ends. Using the Vs as guidelines, with a long serrated knife, cut a V-shaped wedge from the top of the cake. Carefully lift the wedge out of the cake and place it flat side down on a work surface. Using a pastry brush, soak the entire cut surfaces of the two pieces of cake with the sugar syrup.

11. Using a hand-held electric mixer set at medium-high speed, beat the chilled ganache just until it begins to form soft peaks, 30–60 seconds. Do not overbeat, or the ganache will get grainy. Using a metal cake spatula, fill the V-shaped well in the cake with the whipped ganache, smoothing it so that it is level with the top of the cake. Replace the V-shaped wedge flat side down so the top of the cake is now pointed. Press the wedge onto the ganache to adhere. Using the spatula, smooth any ganache that oozes from the sides of the cake. Wrap the cake tightly in plastic wrap and refrigerate until the filling is firm, 1–2 hours, or freeze for about 45 minutes.

12. Place the cake on a wire rack set over a baking sheet. If the remaining ganache has thickened, rewarm it over hot, not simmering, water until it melts enough to pour. Pour the ganache over the top and sides of the cake, spreading it evenly with a metal cake spatula. Refrigerate the cake until the glaze is set, about 10 minutes.

13. Sift the cocoa over the cake, tilting the cake so the entire surface is covered. With a sharp knife, cut a crosshatch pattern over the top of the cake. Keep the cake refrigerated for up to 30 minutes before serving. Using a sharp, thin-bladed knife, cut the cake crosswise into slices about 1 inch thick.

Makes 8 servings

Chocolate Morsels: The unfrosted, unfilled genoise is easiest to cut if made 1 day ahead, wrapped tightly in plastic wrap, and stored at room temperature. The cake can also be frozen, well wrapped in plastic wrap and foil, for up to 1 month. Defrost completely before cutting.

Rigo Jansci

Named for a famous violinist who took Europe by storm, these gorgeously glazed slices of ganache-filled cake are a supreme example of the pastrymaker's art.

CAKE

3 ounces unsweetened chocolate, chopped fine
12 tablespoons (1½ sticks) unsalted butter, softened
½ cup granulated sugar, divided
4 large eggs, separated, at room temperature
1 teaspoon vanilla extract
⅛ teaspoon salt
½ cup cake flour

GANACHE

1½ cups heavy (whipping) cream
12 ounces bittersweet chocolate, chopped fine
2 tablespoons Cognac

⅔ cup apricot preserves

SHINY GLAZE

½ cup water
½ cup granulated sugar
3 tablespoons unsalted butter
½ cup plus 1 tablespoon Dutch-process cocoa powder, such as Droste
½ teaspoon vanilla extract

1. *Make the cake:* Position a rack in the center of the oven and preheat to 350°F. Lightly butter an 11″ × 17″ × 1″ jelly-roll pan. Line the bottom of the pan with a rectangle of wax paper. Dust the sides of the pan with flour, tapping out excess.

2. In the top part of a double boiler over hot, not simmering, water, melt the chocolate, stirring often, until smooth. Remove the top part of the double boiler from the bottom and let stand until the chocolate is tepid, about 10 minutes.

3. In a medium bowl, using a hand-held electric mixer set at high speed, beat the butter until creamy, about 1 minute. Still beating, gradually add ¼ cup of the sugar and beat until the mixture is light in color and consistency, about 2 minutes. Beat in the egg yolks, then the vanilla and salt.

4. In another medium bowl, using a hand-held electric mixer set at low speed, with clean, dry beaters, beat the egg whites until foamy. Increase the speed to high and gradually beat in the remaining ¼ cup sugar, beating until the whites form stiff, shiny peaks.

5. Stir about one-fourth of the beaten whites into the chocolate batter to lighten it. Pour the remaining whites over the batter. Sift the flour over the whites. Using a rubber spatula, fold the ingredients together until combined. Transfer the batter to the prepared pan. Using an offset cake spatula, spread the batter evenly, being sure to fill the corners of the pan.

6. Bake until a toothpick inserted in the center of the cake comes out clean, 15–20 minutes. Cool the cake on a wire cake rack for 10 minutes. Run a sharp knife around the inside of the pan to release the cake from the sides. Invert the cake onto the rack, carefully peel off the wax paper, and cool completely.

7. *Make the ganache:* In a medium saucepan over low heat, bring the cream to a low simmer. Remove the pan from the heat and add the chocolate and cognac. Let stand for 5 minutes to soften the chocolate, then whisk until smooth. Transfer the mixture to a medium bowl set in a larger bowl of ice water. Let the mixture stand until cooled and thickened but not firm, about 10 minutes. Whisk the ganache just until soft peaks form. Do not overbeat the ganache, or it will become grainy.

8. Cut the cake in half vertically to make two 8½″ × 11″ rectangles. Place one layer on a rimless baking sheet. In a small saucepan, bring the preserves to a simmer over medium heat. Rub the preserves through a wire strainer into a small bowl. Using a metal cake spatula, spread the preserves evenly over the layer on the baking sheet. Carefully spread the layer evenly with the ganache, then top with the second layer. Cover the cake loosely with plastic wrap, then refrigerate until the ganache is firm, about 1 hour.

9. *Make the glaze:* In a small saucepan, bring the water, sugar, and butter to a boil over medium heat, stirring constantly, until the sugar is dissolved. Remove from the heat and whisk in the cocoa and vanilla.

10. *Assemble the cake:* Using a serrated knife, trim the edges of the cake and filling. Slide the cake onto a large cake rack set over a wax paper–lined baking sheet. Pour the warm glaze onto the top of the cake. (The warm glaze

will firm when it hits the cold cake, so work quickly.) Using a metal cake spatula, spread the glaze evenly over the top of the cake, letting the excess run down the sides. Smooth the sides of the cake. Refrigerate the cake on the rack until the glaze is set, about 30 minutes.

11. Using a sharp, thin knife dipped in hot water and dried between slices, cut the cake into 16 rectangles. Transfer the cake slices to a serving platter. (The cake can be prepared up to 1 day ahead, covered loosely with plastic wrap, and refrigerated.)

Makes 16 servings

Chocolate Morsels: If you don't have a rimless baking sheet, you can place the cake on an upturned rimmed baking sheet. When you transfer the cake to the rack, slip a large spatula under it for support.

Chocolate Bûche de Noël

Christmas in France means the bakeries will be filled with bûches de Noël, cake roulades decorated to represent the logs on a winter hearth. I present the log on a bed of chocolate twigs (available at many specialty grocers) and decorate it with leaves and truffles to make an impressive trompe l'oeil *effect.*

CHOCOLATE ROLL
6 large eggs, separated, at room
    temperature
¼ teaspoon cream of tartar
¾ cup granulated sugar, divided
⅓ cup plus 2 tablespoons Dutch-
    process cocoa powder, such as
    Droste, sifted

FILLING
1 teaspoon unflavored gelatin
2 tablespoons boiling water
1½ cups heavy (whipping) cream
2 tablespoons confectioners' sugar
½ teaspoon vanilla extract

GANACHE
½ cup heavy (whipping) cream
6 ounces bittersweet chocolate,
    chopped fine
1 tablespoon dark rum or cognac
    (optional)

GARNISH
2 tablespoons Dutch-process cocoa
    powder, such as Droste
1 4.3-ounce box bittersweet
    chocolate twigs
Chocolate leaves (see Index)
Grand Marnier Truffles (see
    Index)

1. *Make the chocolate roll:* Position a rack in the center of the oven and preheat to 350°F. Lightly butter a 10½″ × 15½″ × 1″ jelly-roll pan. To line the bottom and sides of the pan, cut a 12″ × 16″ piece of parchment paper or wax paper. At each of the four corners, cut a diagonal slash about 2 inches long. Fit the parchment paper into the pan, folding the cut ends over each other at the slashes to form neat corners. Lightly butter the parchment paper and dust with flour, tapping out excess.

2. In a large grease-free bowl, using a hand-held electric mixer set at low speed, with clean, dry beaters, beat the egg whites until foamy. Add the cream of tartar, increase the speed to medium-high, and beat until soft peaks begin to form. Gradually add ¼ cup of the sugar and continue beating until stiff peaks form.

3. In another large bowl, using a hand-held electric mixer set at high speed, beat the egg yolks with ⅓ cup of the cocoa and the remaining ½ cup sugar until the mixture forms a thick, slowly dissolving ribbon when the beaters are lifted 2 inches above the mixture, about 2 minutes. Stir about one-fourth of the beaten whites into the yolk mixture to lighten it. Using a rubber spatula, fold in the remaining whites.

4. Scrape the batter into the prepared pan and spread evenly with a metal cake spatula, preferably offset. Bake for 12–15 minutes, until the center of the cake springs back when touched lightly with a finger. Cool completely in the pan on a wire cake rack. Sift the remaining 2 tablespoons cocoa over the top of the cake.

5. *Make the filling:* In a small bowl, sprinkle the gelatin over the boiling water. Let stand for 5 minutes, then stir well to dissolve the gelatin. In a chilled medium bowl, using a hand-held electric mixer set at medium-high speed, beat the heavy cream until soft peaks begin to form. Add the confectioners' sugar, vanilla, and dissolved gelatin and beat just until stiff.

6. Place a large sheet of aluminum foil over the top of the cake. Place a large cutting board or baking sheet over the pan. Invert the cake and foil onto the platter. Carefully peel off the parchment paper.

7. Spread the cake evenly with the filling, leaving a 1-inch border around the edges. Using the foil as an aid, beginning at a long end, roll the cake into a tight cylinder. (The roll can be wrapped tightly in the foil and refrigerated for up to 1 day before frosting.)

8. *Make the ganache:* In a small saucepan over low heat, bring the heavy cream to a simmer. Remove from the heat and add the chocolate and the liquor if desired. Let stand for 5 minutes, then whisk until smooth. Transfer to a medium bowl set in a larger bowl of ice water. Let stand, stirring often, until well chilled and thickened, 5–10 minutes. Whisk the mixture just until stiff peaks begin to form. Do not overbeat, or the ganache will become grainy. Immediately spread the top and sides of the roll with the ganache. With the tines of a fork, make wavy lines along the surface of the ganache to simulate bark. (The frosted roll can be prepared up to 1 day ahead, covered with plastic wrap, and refrigerated.)

9. *Garnish the cake:* Sprinkle the top of the roll with the cocoa. Garnish the roll with the chocolate twigs, leaves, and truffles.

Makes 8–12 servings

Chocolate Morsels: If the chocolate twigs are unavailable, garnish the platter with sprigs of fresh, nontoxic evergreens, such as juniper or pine. Do not use holly or poinsettia—both are poisonous.

Grand Indulgence Hot Chocolate

A couple of years ago I was invited to be the guest chef at the Great American Chocolate Festival at Hershey, Pennsylvania, where I devised this suave hot chocolate for grown-ups. At my booth in the Chocolate Gallery, a bazaar of various chocolate offerings, I served more than 1,000 portions in under 2 hours. After one sip you'll know why they lined up for this one! The recipe is based on the European way to make hot chocolate—blending melted bittersweet chocolate instead of cocoa with hot milk. Of course, when you make the drink for youngsters, omit the liqueur.

1¼ cups hot milk
Zest of ½ small orange, removed
    with a vegetable peeler
1 cinnamon stick
1 ounce bittersweet or semisweet
    chocolate
2 tablespoons Grand Marnier or
    other orange-flavored liqueur
Sweetened whipped cream for
    garnish (optional)

1. In a small saucepan, combine the hot milk, orange zest, and cinnamon stick. Bring to a low simmer over very low heat. Let the mixture stand for 5 minutes. Reheat to a low simmer. With a slotted spoon, remove and discard the orange zest and cinnamon stick.

2. In a blender, process the chocolate, Grand Marnier, and hot milk until smooth. Pour into a coffee mug and serve immediately, topped with whipped cream if desired.

Makes 1 serving

Chocolate Morsels: This drink is also spectacular with dark rum or cognac replacing the Grand Marnier. You may delete steeping the orange zest in the milk if you wish.

Tropical Chocolate Fondue with Seasonal Fruits

❦

Fondue is a fun-filled way to entertain close friends. This chocolate fondue has a particularly interesting coconut accent, making it almost like a liquid candy bar.

1 12-ounce can cream of coconut, such as Coco Lopez
12 ounces bittersweet chocolate, chopped fine
Seasonal fresh fruit, such as fresh pineapple chunks, halved and pitted apricots, hulled strawberries, and orange segments
1 small store-bought pound cake, cut into 1-inch cubes
½ cup sweetened coconut flakes
2 ounces slivered blanched almonds, chopped coarse (about ½ cup)

1. In a medium saucepan, bring the cream of coconut to a low simmer over medium heat. Remove the saucepan from the heat, add the chocolate, and let stand for 5 minutes, until the chocolate is melted. Whisk until smooth. (The chocolate sauce can be made up to 2 days ahead, covered, and refrigerated. Reheat in the fondue pot.)

2. Transfer the sauce to a fondue pot or chafing dish and serve warm. Arrange the fresh fruit and cake cubes on a large platter and place the coconut and almonds in small bowls. Use fondue forks for dipping the fruit into the sauce, letting guests sprinkle coconut or almonds on their serving.

Makes 6-8 servings

Chocolate French Toast

If you are a true chocolate fan, you are always looking for ways to get a little extra chocolate into your life. Here's one way to make the day ahead much more pleasant.

5 ounces semisweet chocolate,
   grated coarse
1 loaf (about 9 ounces) French or
   Italian bread, sliced into 24
   ½-inch slices
3 large eggs
1 cup half-and-half
2 tablespoons granulated sugar
1 tablespoon unsalted butter
1 tablespoon vegetable oil
Maple syrup, warmed, for serving

1. Preheat the oven to 200°F. sprinkle about 2 tablespoons of the grated chocolate evenly over each of 12 bread slices. Place the remaining 12 slices on top to make 12 sandwiches.

2. In a medium bowl, whisk together the eggs, half-and-half, and sugar. In a large nonstick skillet, melt the butter and vegetable oil over medium-high heat until very hot. Reduce the heat to medium. Quickly dip one of the sandwiches in the egg mixture and place it in the skillet. Repeat with five more sandwiches. Cook until golden brown on each side, turning once, about 6 minutes altogether. Transfer the French toast to a baking sheet and keep it warm in the oven. Repeat the procedure with the remaining sandwiches, adding additional butter and oil if necessary. Serve the French toast immediately with the warm maple syrup passed on the side.

Makes 4–6 servings

White Chocolate Coeur à la Crème

A delectable cream cheese and white chocolate mixture molded into a heart shape, this is a show-stopping finale to a Valentine's Day dinner. Lovely white porcelain coeur à la crème molds are easily acquired at specialty food shops and can be displayed prominently on your kitchen wall as ornaments when they aren't in use.

COEUR A LA CREME
9 ounces imported high-quality white chocolate, chopped fine
12 ounces cream cheese, softened
½ cup plus 2 tablespoons sour cream
½ cup plus 2 tablespoons heavy (whipping) cream
3 tablespoons white crème de cacao or additional heavy cream

RASPBERRY SAUCE
2 cups fresh or defrosted frozen raspberries
¼ cup superfine sugar or to taste
3 tablespoons raspberry liqueur, such as Chambord (optional)
2 teaspoons fresh lemon juice or to taste

1. *Make the coeur à la crème:* In the top part of a double boiler over hot, not simmering, water, melt about half of the white chocolate, stirring often, until almost completely melted. Add the remaining white chocolate and continue melting and stirring often until smooth. Remove the top part of the double boiler from the bottom. Let the chocolate stand, stirring often, until tepid, about 10 minutes.

2. In a medium bowl, using a hand-held electric mixer set at medium-high speed, beat the cream cheese until smooth, about 1 minute. Add the sour cream, heavy cream, and crème de cacao. Add the cooled white chocolate. Beat just until well mixed and lump-free.

3. Line a 4- to 5-cup coeur à la crème mold with a piece of cheesecloth that has been rinsed and squeezed dry, letting the excess cheesecloth hang over the sides of the mold. Spoon the cheese mixture into the prepared mold and spread evenly. Fold the excess cheesecloth over the top of the cheese. Place the mold on a baking sheet and refrigerate for at least 6 hours or overnight.

4. Discard the whey that has collected on the baking sheet. Peel back the cheesecloth. Place a serving dish on top of the mold and invert the two together to unmold. Peel off the cheesecloth.

5. *Make the raspberry sauce:* In a food processor fitted with the metal blade, puree the raspberries, sugar, liqueur if desired, and lemon juice until smooth. Using a wooden spoon, strain and rub the sauce through a wire strainer into a small bowl, discarding the seeds.

6. Cut the coeur à la crème into slices and serve chilled with raspberry sauce. (The coeur à la crème and the raspberry sauce can be prepared up to 2 days ahead, covered, and refrigerated. The longer the coeur stands, the firmer it will become.)

Makes 6 servings

Chocolate-Dipped Orange Cookies

Enjoy these plump goodies with a nice cup of hot chocolate. A fireplace and a good book are optional.

⅓ cup finely chopped candied
    orange peel
3 tablespoons Grand Marnier,
    other orange-flavored liqueur,
    or orange juice
1½ cups all-purpose flour
½ teaspoon baking powder
¼ teaspoon salt
8 tablespoons (1 stick) unsalted
    butter, softened
½ cup granulated sugar
½ cup packed light brown sugar
2 large eggs, at room temperature
½ teaspoon vanilla extract
2 ounces pecans, toasted (see
    Index) and chopped fine (about
    ½ cup)
4 ounces milk chocolate, chopped
    fine

1. In a small bowl, soak the candied peel in the orange liqueur for 30 minutes; do not drain.

2. Position two racks in the top and bottom thirds of the oven and preheat to 375°F. In a medium bowl, stir together the flour, baking powder, and salt.

3. In another medium bowl, using a hand-held electric mixer set at high speed, beat the butter until creamy, about 1 minute. Gradually add the sugars and beat until light in color and consistency, about 2 minutes. One at a time, beat in the eggs and then the vanilla. Using a wooden spoon, stir in the flour mixture, then the pecans and the orange peel with liquid.

4. Drop the batter by level tablespoons, about 1½ inches apart, onto ungreased baking sheets. Bake, switching the baking sheets from the top rack to the bottom rack halfway through baking, until the cookies spring back when pressed lightly in the center, 8–10 minutes. Let the cookies cool on the baking sheets for 5 minutes. Transfer them to wire cake racks to cool completely.

5. In the top part of a double boiler over hot, not simmering, water, melt the chocolate, stirring often, until smooth. Remove the top part of the double boiler from the bottom.

6. Tilt the top part of the double boiler so that the melted chocolate collects in a pool on one side. Dip half of each cookie into the melted chocolate. Scrape the bottom of the cookie on the edge of the double boiler insert to remove any excess chocolate. Place the cookie on a wire rack set over a baking sheet. Repeat the procedure with the remaining cookies. Refrigerate the cookies on the rack until the chocolate is set, about 5 minutes. The cookies will keep for up to 3 days stored between sheets of wax paper in an airtight container at room temperature.

Makes about 36 cookies

Tiramisù

Tiramisù is the current darling of Italian restaurant dessert tables, and no wonder. This marvelously creamy dessert is rumored to have revitalizing properties—hence its name, which means "pick-me-up." No doubt about it: one spoonful will revitalize a flagging spirit. There is no "official" tiramisù recipe, so if my rendition isn't a carbon copy of your favorite trattoria's version, I can only shrug my shoulders, Italian style. For example, tiramisù can be made with ladyfingers, sponge cake, or, as here, chocolate cake. Italians make theirs with mascarpone, a very delicate fresh cheese that is hard to find in America except in urban areas with large Italian populations. When you do locate it, it's pretty expensive. Some U.S. restaurants approximate mascarpone with a sweet custard sauce, but I use a blend of ricotta, cream cheese, and heavy cream.

CHOCOLATE CAKE
1 cup all-purpose flour
⅓ cup nonalkalized cocoa powder,
   such as Hershey's
¼ teaspoon baking soda
½ teaspoon salt
12 tablespoons (1½ sticks) unsalted
   butter, softened
1 cup granulated sugar
½ cup packed light brown sugar
3 large eggs, at room temperature
1 teaspoon vanilla extract
½ cup milk

ESPRESSO SYRUP
½ cup strong brewed coffee,
   preferably espresso
¼ cup dark rum, cognac, or
   additional brewed coffee
1 tablespoon confectioners' sugar

CHEESE FILLING
3 cups whole-milk ricotta
1 pound cream cheese, softened
¾ cup heavy (whipping) cream
¾ cup confectioners' sugar

1 tablespoon Dutch-process cocoa
   powder, such as Droste
1 ounce bittersweet chocolate,
   grated

1. *Make the cake:* Position a rack in the center of the oven and preheat to 350°F. Lightly butter the inside of an 8″ × 4″ loaf pan. Line the bottom of

the pan with a rectangle of wax paper. Dust the inside of the pan with flour, tapping out excess flour.

2. Sift together the flour, cocoa, baking soda, and salt through a wire strainer onto a piece of wax paper. In a medium bowl, using a hand-held electric mixer set at high speed, beat the butter until creamy, about 1 minute. Gradually add the granulated and brown sugars and beat until light in color and consistency, about 2 minutes. One at a time, beat in the eggs, beating well after each addition. Beat in the vanilla. A third at a time, alternately add the flour mixture and milk, beating well after each addition and scraping down the sides of the bowl as necessary. Transfer the batter to the prepared pan, smoothing the top with a rubber spatula.

3. Bake until a toothpick inserted in the center of the cake comes out clean, 60–70 minutes. Cool the cake completely in the pan on a wire cake rack. Run a sharp knife around the edge of the cake to loosen it from the sides, then invert the cake onto the cake rack. Carefully peel off the wax paper.

4. *Make the syrup:* In a small bowl, stir together the coffee, rum, and confectioners' sugar until the sugar is dissolved.

5. *Make the filling:* In a food processor fitted with the metal blade, process the ricotta cheese until smooth. Add the cream cheese, heavy cream, and confectioners' sugar; process until well combined.

6. *Assemble the dessert:* Slice the cake crosswise into ½-inch-thick slices. Line the bottom of a 7″ × 11″ (2 quart) baking dish with half of the cake slices. (The slices don't have to fit exactly, and they can overlap if necessary.) Sprinkle the slices with half of the espresso syrup. Using a rubber spatula, spread the soaked cake slices with half of the cheese filling. Repeat the layering with the remaining cake slices, espresso syrup, and cheese filling. Cover the tiramisù with plastic wrap and refrigerate to allow the flavors to blend, at least 2 hours or overnight. (The tiramisù can be prepared up to 1 day ahead, covered, and refrigerated.)

7. Just before serving, sift the cocoa through a wire strainer over the top of the tiramisù and sprinkle with the grated chocolate. To serve, spoon the tiramisù into dessert bowls.

Makes 6–8 servings

Spuma di Caffé Latte

I've updated a popular "mousse in a blender" recipe from the not-so-distant culinary past, as tasty to eat as it is speedy to prepare. To emphasize my coffeehouse inspiration for the dessert, I like serving the espresso-flavored mousse in coffee cups topped with big swirls of whipped cream.

7 ounces bittersweet chocolate, broken up
2 large eggs, well beaten
¾ cup milk
¾ teaspoon instant espresso powder
3 tablespoons boiling water

1 tablespoon dark rum, cognac, or Kahlúa (optional)
½ cup heavy (whipping) cream
1 tablespoon confectioners' sugar
Ground cinnamon or unsweetened cocoa powder for garnish

1. Place the chocolate in a blender or a food processor fitted with the metal blade.

2. In a small saucepan, whisk the eggs well. Gradually whisk in the milk. Using a wooden spoon, stir constantly over medium-low heat until the mixture is thick enough to lightly coat the back of the spoon, 3–4 minutes. (An instant-read thermometer inserted into the mixture will read about 175°F.) Do not let the custard boil. With the food processor running, slowly pour the hot custard through the feed tube and process until smooth.

3. In a small bowl, dissolve the espresso powder in the boiling water. Add the espresso mixture and the rum to the mousse and pulse until combined. Transfer the mousse to four coffee cups and smooth the tops. Cover each cup with plastic wrap and refrigerate until the mousse is firm, at least 2 hours or overnight.

4. Just before serving, in a chilled medium bowl, using a hand-held electric mixer set at high speed, whip the heavy cream just until soft peaks form. Beat in the confectioners' sugar. Spoon dollops of the whipped cream over each mousse, sprinkle lightly with cinnamon or cocoa, and serve immediately.

Makes 4 servings

8
Bow-Tie Desserts

Bittersweet Lemon Tart
Chocolate Walnut Tart
White Chocolate–Pistachio Tea Bread
Chocolate Orange Mousse Pie
White Chocolate Celebration Cake
White Chocolate Passion Fruit Tart
Berry and Chocolate Sandwich
Raspberry-Topped Fudge Tart
San Andreas Fudge Torte
Irish Cream–Chip Cheesecake

Bittersweet Lemon Tart

Chocolate and lemon make a felicitous match in this lovely tart. Decorated with chocolate leaves (easily molded from fresh lemon leaves, available at most florists), it is a taste tingling salute to bittersweet flavors and was a big hit with my friends.

CRUST
8 tablespoons (1 stick) unsalted
    butter, softened
½ cup granulated sugar
2 large egg yolks
1¼ cups all-purpose flour
3 ounces bittersweet chocolate,
    chopped fine

FILLING
1 cup granulated sugar
2 large eggs
2 tablespoons all-purpose flour
2 tablespoons fresh lemon juice
Grated zest of 1 lemon
Chocolate leaves for garnish (see
    Index)

1. *Make the crust:* Position a rack in the top third of the oven and preheat to 375°F. Lightly butter a 9-inch round fluted tart pan with a removable bottom.

2. In a medium bowl, using a hand-held electric mixer set at high speed, beat the butter until creamy. Gradually add the sugar and beat until the mixture is light in color and consistency. Beat in the egg yolks. Using a wooden spoon, stir in the flour to make a soft dough. Press the dough firmly and evenly into the bottom and up the sides of the prepared pan. Prick the dough well with a fork.

3. Bake for 10 minutes. Deflate any air bubbles in the crust by pricking with a fork, then continue baking until the crust is lightly browned, about 10 minutes longer. Cool the pastry shell for 2 minutes, then sprinkle it with the chopped chocolate. Let stand for about 5 minutes, until the chocolate is softened. Using the back of a spoon, spread the chocolate evenly on the bottom and up the sides of the shell. Set the pan on a baking sheet.

4. *Make the filling:* In a medium bowl, using a hand-held electric mixer set at medium speed, beat the sugar, eggs, flour, lemon juice, and zest until well combined, about 1 minute. Pour the lemon filling into the tart pan.

5. Bake for 20–25 minutes, until the top of the filling is lightly browned. (The filling will not be completely set.) Cool the tart completely on a wire cake rack. Lift up the bottom of the tart pan from the sides. Just before serving, garnish the top of the tart with the chocolate leaves arranged in a spoke pattern. (The tart can be prepared up to 1 day ahead, covered with plastic wrap, and refrigerated.)

Makes 8 servings

Chocolate Walnut Tart

Thanks to Diane Kniss for this recipe from her Saugerties, New York, catering business, Baked Goods in High Woods. The sweet tart shell is slathered with chocolate, sprinkled with big chunks of walnuts, and filled with a caramel concoction. Drizzled with more chocolate, it is pretty enough for the finest restaurant dessert cart, but now you can serve it at home.

PASTRY SHELL
1 cup all-purpose flour
2 tablespoons granulated sugar
⅛ teaspoon salt
5 tablespoons unsalted butter,
   chilled and cut into pieces
1 large egg yolk, chilled
2 tablespoons ice water
3 ounces bittersweet chocolate,
   finely chopped

FILLING
1 cup granulated sugar
¼ cup water
¾ cup heavy (whipping) cream,
   scalded and kept hot
3 tablespoons unsalted butter,
   melted
1 large egg, beaten
¾ teaspoon vanilla extract
6 ounces walnuts, chopped coarse
   (about 1½ cups)

1 ounce bittersweet chocolate,
   chopped fine, for garnish

1. *Make the pastry shell:* In a medium bowl, stir together the flour, sugar, and salt. Add the butter pieces. Using a pastry blender or two knives, cut in the butter until the mixture resembles coarse meal. In a small bowl, stir together the egg yolk and ice water. Tossing the flour-butter mixture with a fork, sprinkle it with the liquids, tossing just until moistened and the dough holds together when pinched between your thumb and forefinger. (You may have to sprinkle in more water, 1 teaspoon at a time.) Gather the dough into a thick disk and wrap it in wax paper. Refrigerate for at least 1 hour or overnight.

2. On a lightly floured work surface, roll out the dough into a 13-inch circle about ⅛ inch thick. Ease the dough carefully into a buttered 9-inch round fluted tart pan with a removable bottom. Fold in the edges of the dough to make a double layer of dough around the sides and press it against the sides of the pan, making sure there are no air pockets. Trim the excess dough by pressing it against the fluted edge. With a fork, prick the bottom of the dough. Line the inside of the pastry-filled pan with aluminum foil and place in the freezer for 30 minutes.

3. Position a rack in the bottom third of the oven and preheat to 375°F. Weight the foil-lined dough with dry beans or rice. Bake for about 10 minutes, until the dough is set. Remove the foil and beans and continue baking until the shell is lightly browned, about 15 minutes longer. Cool the pastry shell for 2 minutes and then sprinkle with the 3 ounces of finely chopped chocolate. Let stand for 5 minutes, until the chocolate is softened. Using the back of a spoon, spread the chocolate evenly on the bottom and up the sides of the shell. Cool the shell on a wire cake rack while making the filling.

4. *Make the filling:* Meanwhile, in a tall, medium saucepan over high heat, bring the sugar and water to a boil, stirring constantly. Stop stirring and boil the syrup until golden brown, about 5 minutes. Gradually stir in the hot scalded cream. (The mixture will bubble, so be careful.) Reduce the heat to medium-low and simmer for 3 minutes. Remove the pan from the heat and let cool completely, about 1 hour. Whisk in the melted butter, egg, and vanilla until smooth. Arrange the walnuts in the chocolate-lined shell. Pour the filling over the walnuts. Place the tart on a baking sheet.

5. Increase the oven temperature to 400°F. Bake the tart for 15 minutes. Reduce the heat to 350°F and continue baking until the filling is bubbling in the center of the tart, about 15 minutes longer. Cool the tart completely on a wire cake rack.

6. In the top part of a double boiler over hot, not simmering, water, melt the remaining ounce of chocolate, stirring often, until smooth. Transfer the melted chocolate to a small plastic bag. Let cool for 10 minutes, until tepid. Squeeze the melted chocolate into one corner of the bag. Using scissors, snip a ⅛-inch opening off the corner. Squeeze and drizzle the melted chocolate over the surface of the tart. Refrigerate the tart for 10 minutes to set the drizzle. (The tart can be made up to 1 day ahead and stored at room temperature.)

Makes 8 servings

Chocolate Morsels: To make Chocolate Cashew Tart, substitute 1½ cups unsalted cashews (available at natural foods stores) for the walnuts. Use milk chocolate instead of bittersweet chocolate.

Two very important tips:

The caramel filling has a tendency to boil over unless you choose a saucepan deep enough, such as a tall 2-quart saucepan. Minimize boiling over by adding the cream *gradually*.

Be sure that you add hot scalded cream to the cooked syrup, because chilled cream will make the syrup harden and not incorporate properly.

White Chocolate–Pistachio Tea Bread

A refreshing citrus note adds contrast to the sweetness of white chocolate in this tender pound cake. Pistachio nuts contribute their crunch and subtle flavor, but it's their green color, accenting the ivory-hued loaf, that I like most. In short, this is the nicest way I can think of to get lemon in your tea.

BREAD

3 ounces (about ¾ cup) shelled pistachios
1 tablespoon unsalted butter, melted
2 tablespoons dried bread crumbs
2 ounces high-quality imported white chocolate, chopped fine
1½ cups cake flour
½ teaspoon baking soda
¼ teaspoon salt
8 tablespoons (1 stick) unsalted butter, softened
1 cup granulated sugar
Grated zest of 1 lemon
1¼ teaspoons vanilla extract
¼ teaspoon almond extract
3 large eggs, beaten, at room temperature
½ cup plain low-fat yogurt, at room temperature

GLAZE

¼ cup heavy (whipping) cream
2 tablespoons unsalted butter
6 ounces high-quality imported white chocolate, chopped fine
1½ teaspoons fresh lemon juice
Grated zest of 1 lemon

1. *Make the tea bread:* In a medium saucepan of boiling water, cook the pistachios for 2 minutes, then drain well and rinse under cold water. While the nuts are still warm, slip off the skins between your fingers. Place the nuts in a single layer on a baking sheet and let dry at room temperature for at least 3 hours.

2. Position a rack in the center of the oven and preheat to 350°F. Bake the nuts for 6–8 minutes, shaking the pan a couple of times, until fragrant but not browned. Cool the pistachios completely, then chop coarse.

3. Brush the bottom and sides of a 9″ × 5″ loaf pan with the melted butter. Dust the bottom and sides of the pan with the crumbs, tapping out excess.

4. In the top part of a double boiler over hot, not simmering, water, melt the white chocolate, stirring often, until smooth. Remove the top part of the double boiler from the bottom and cool the chocolate for about 10 minutes, until tepid.

5. Sift the flour, baking soda, and salt together through a wire strainer onto a sheet of wax paper. In a large bowl, using a hand-held electric mixer set at medium speed, beat the butter until creamy, about 30 seconds. Gradually beat in the sugar. Beat in the lemon zest and vanilla and almond extracts. Scrape down the sides of the bowl and slowly beat in the eggs. Continue beating for about 2 minutes, until the mixture is light and fluffy. (The mixture may look slightly curdled.) Beat in the tepid white chocolate.

6. At low speed, one-half at a time, alternately beat in the yogurt and flour mixture, scraping down the sides of the bowl as necessary with a rubber spatula. Using a wooden spoon, stir in ½ cup plus 2 tablespoons of the chopped pistachios. Scrape the batter into the prepared pan and smooth the top with the spatula.

7. Bake until a toothpick inserted in the center of the loaf comes out clean, 50–60 minutes. Cool the loaf for 10 minutes on a wire cake rack. Run a knife around the edges of the bread to loosen and invert the bread onto the rack. Turn the loaf right side up and cool completely.

8. *Make the glaze:* In a medium saucepan over medium-low heat, bring the cream and butter to a low simmer. Remove the pan from the heat and add the white chocolate. Let stand for 2 minutes, then whisk until smooth. Whisk in the lemon juice and zest. Let stand for about 10 minutes, until thickened but still pourable.

9. Place the cooled bread on a wire rack set over a wax paper-lined work surface. Pour the glaze over the bread. Using a metal cake spatula, spread the glaze evenly over the top of the bread, letting the excess run down the sides. Smooth the glaze over the sides of the bread, scooping up excess glaze from the wax paper to cover any bare spots. Sprinkle the remaining 2 tablespoons chopped pistachios in a line down the center of the bread. Refrigerate the bread for about 20 minutes to set the glaze. (The bread can be prepared up to 1 day ahead, covered, and stored at room temperature.)

Makes 8 servings

Chocolate Orange Mousse Pie

I can't resist the heady combination of orange and chocolate! And it's especially delicious in this dessert—a kissin' cousin to a classic chiffon pie, but with an extra measure of savoir faire from a dash of Grand Marnier.

CRUST
1⅓ cups (about 6 ounces) crushed
   chocolate wafer cookies
¼ cup granulated sugar
4 tablespoons (½ stick) unsalted
   butter, melted

MOUSSE
1 envelope (about 2½ teaspoons)
   unflavored gelatin
2 tablespoons boiling water
2 large eggs, separated, at room
   temperature
½ cup granulated sugar, divided
¼ teaspoon salt
1 cup milk
6 ounces bittersweet chocolate,
   chopped fine
3 tablespoons Grand Marnier or
   other orange-flavored liqueur
Grated zest of 1 orange
½ cup heavy (whipping) cream

TOPPING
¾ cup heavy (whipping) cream
2 tablespoons confectioners' sugar
1 tablespoon Grand Marnier or
   other orange-flavored liqueur
Chocolate curls for garnish
   (optional; see Index)

1. *Make the crust:* Butter the sides and bottom of a 9-inch round pie plate. In a medium bowl, mix together the cookie crumbs, sugar, and melted butter until combined. Press the mixture evenly onto the bottom and sides of the prepared pan. Refrigerate the crust while you make the chocolate mousse.

2. *Make the mousse:* In a small bowl, sprinkle the gelatin over the boiling water and let it stand for 5 minutes, until softened.

3. In a large bowl, whisk together the egg yolks, ¼ cup of the sugar, and the salt. In a heavy-bottomed medium saucepan, bring the milk to a simmer over medium-low heat. Gradually whisk the hot milk into the yolk mixture. Return the mixture to the saucepan, then whisk in the softened gelatin. Stirring constantly with a wooden spoon, cook the custard until the gelatin is dissolved, about 1 minute. (The custard will not coat the spoon.) Remove the pan from the heat and add the chocolate. Let stand for 2 minutes to melt the chocolate, then whisk until smooth. Whisk in the Grand Marnier and orange zest.

4. Return the custard to the large bowl, set in a larger bowl of ice water. Let the mixture stand until cooled and just beginning to set, about 10 minutes. Remove the custard from the ice water.

5. In a medium-size grease-free bowl, using a hand-held electric mixer set at low speed, with clean, dry beaters, beat the egg whites until foamy. Increase the speed to high and continue beating just until the whites form soft peaks. Gradually beat in the remaining ¼ cup sugar and continue beating until the whites form stiff, shiny peaks. Using a rubber spatula, stir about one-third of the whites into the chocolate mixture to lighten it, then fold in the remaining whites.

6. In a chilled medium bowl, using a hand-held electric mixer set at high speed, beat the heavy cream just until soft peaks begin to form. Stir about one-fourth of the whipped cream into the chocolate mixture, then fold in the remaining cream.

7. Return the bowl of the chocolate mixture to the bowl of ice water (add fresh ice cubes if necessary). Chill, folding occasionally with a rubber spatula, until beginning to set, about 20 minutes. Spoon the mixture into the crust, cover loosely with plastic wrap, and refrigerate until the mousse is firm, at least 2 hours or overnight.

8. *Make the topping:* In a chilled, large bowl, using a hand-held electric mixer set at high speed, beat the cream until soft peaks begin to form. Add the confectioners' sugar and Grand Marnier and beat until stiff peaks form. Using a metal spatula, spread the cream over the filling. Garnish with chocolate curls if desired. (The pie can be prepared up to 1 day ahead, covered loosely with plastic wrap, and refrigerated.)

Makes 6–8 servings

White Chocolate Celebration Cake

This frilly, feminine cake was designed with a Mother's Day celebration in mind. Its ivory white buttercream frosting cloaks a rose-scented chocolate cake, crowned with sparkling glazed garden roses. This pretty-as-a-picture offering would be perfect for a Sweet 16 party, a young lady's graduation, or a baby or bridal shower.

ROSES
1 large egg white
6 unsprayed fresh roses, well
 washed and patted dry
¾ cup superfine sugar

SYRUP
⅓ cup water
⅓ cup granulated sugar
2 tablespoons rose water

GENOISE
½ cup cake flour
½ cup Dutch-process cocoa
 powder, such as Droste
¼ teaspoon salt
8 tablespoons (1 stick) unsalted
 butter
6 large eggs, at room temperature
1 cup granulated sugar
1 teaspoon rose water

BUTTERCREAM
12 ounces high-quality imported
 white chocolate, chopped fine
1½ cups (3 sticks) unsalted butter
 at cool room temperature
1 tablespoon rose water
½ cup confectioners' sugar

1. *Make the candied roses:* In a small bowl, beat the egg white well until foamy. With a small pastry brush, paint each rose with beaten egg white. Frost each with a sprinkling of superfine sugar. Place the candied roses on a wire cake rack and let dry at room temperature overnight.

2. *Make the rose syrup:* In a small saucepan, combine the water and sugar. Cook over medium-low heat, stirring constantly with a wooden spoon, until the sugar dissolves. Increase the heat to medium-high and, without stirring, bring the syrup to a boil. Remove from the heat and cool completely. Stir in the rose water.

3. *Make the genoise:* Position a rack in the center of the oven and preheat to 350°F. Lightly butter two 9-inch round cake pans. Line the bottoms of the pans with rounds of wax paper. Dust the sides of the pans with flour, tapping out excess. Sift the flour, cocoa, and salt together through a wire strainer onto a piece of wax paper.

4. In a small saucepan, bring the butter to a boil over low heat. Pour the melted butter into a glass measuring cup and let stand for 5 minutes. Skim off any foam that is floating on the surface of the melted butter. Pour off the clear yellow melted butter into a small bowl, discarding the milky white solids that have sunk to the bottom of the cup. Set the clarified butter aside.

5. In a large heatproof bowl, whisk together the eggs and sugar until blended. Set the bowl over a medium saucepan of hot, not simmering, water. (The bottom of the bowl must touch the water.) Continue whisking constantly until the sugar is dissolved and the mixture is hot to the touch (110–120°F), about 3 minutes. (Rub a dab of the egg mixture between your thumb and forefinger to feel for any undissolved sugar.) Remove the bowl from the hot water.

6. Using a hand-held electric mixer set at high speed, beat the egg mixture until it is pale yellow and has tripled in volume, about 5 minutes. Beat in the rose water.

7. Resift about one-third of the flour mixture over the batter. Using a large balloon whisk or a rubber spatula, fold in the flour mixture. In two more additions, fold in the remaining flour mixture. (Don't worry if some flour remains visible.)

8. Spoon about one-fourth of the batter into the reserved melted butter and whisk until smooth. Pour the butter mixture into the batter and fold together with the whisk just until combined. Transfer the batter to the prepared pans and smooth the tops with a rubber spatula.

9. Bake until the tops of the cakes spring back when pressed lightly in the center with a finger and the cakes are shrinking from the sides of the pans, 25–30 minutes. Cool the cakes on a wire cake rack for 5 minutes. Run a sharp knife around the edges of the cakes to release them from the sides of the pans. Invert the cakes onto the cake rack and unmold. Carefully peel off the wax paper. Turn the cakes right side up and cool completely. (The cake layers can be prepared up to 2 days ahead, wrapped tightly in plastic wrap, and stored at room temperature, or frozen for up to 1 month.)

10. *Make the buttercream:* In the top part of a double boiler over hot, not simmering, water, heat half of the white chocolate, stirring often, until almost melted. Add the remaining white chocolate and melt, stirring often, until smooth. Remove the top part of the double boiler from the bottom and cool the white chocolate until tepid, about 10 minutes.

11. In a medium bowl, using a hand-held electric mixer set at high speed, beat the butter until creamy, about 1 minute. Add the cooled white chocolate and the rose water and beat until well combined. Reduce the speed to low, add the confectioners' sugar, and beat until thickened. Cover the bowl with plastic wrap and refrigerate until thickened to frosting consistency, 30–45 minutes.

12. *Assemble the cake:* Using a serrated knife, cut the top crusts from the cakes, leveling the tops at the same time. With a dry pastry brush, brush away any excess crumbs from the tops and sides of the cakes.

13. Place one cake layer on a serving platter. Using a pastry brush, soak the layer with half of the syrup. Using a metal cake spatula, spread the layer with about ½ cup of the buttercream, then top with the second layer. Soak the top layer with the remaining syrup. Frost the top and sides of the cake with a very thin layer of buttercream to "set" the crumbs. Refrigerate the cake until the frosting is firm, about 15 minutes. Continue frosting the cake with the remaining frosting, being careful not to disturb the hardened first layer. Garnish the cake with the frosted roses. (The finished cake can be prepared up to 1 day ahead, covered loosely with plastic wrap, and refrigerated. Remove the cake from the refrigerator about 30 minutes before serving.)

Makes 8–10 servings

Chocolate Morsels: While the rose water delicately perfumes the cake in a lovely manner, some bakers may prefer to substitute the fruitier flavor of orange blossom water. (If you are lucky enough to have orange blossoms handy, glaze them to decorate the cake. Otherwise, use the roses.) Both rose water and orange blossom water are available at specialty foods stores and at some pharmacies and gift shops.

White Chocolate Passion Fruit Tart

I am crazy about pairing white chocolate and passion fruit—note the Passionate White Chocolate Truffles in Chapter 6 (see Index). Here I celebrate their happy union with a white chocolate–lined almond crust filled with a tangy passion fruit mousse. The mousse is topped with a sparkling bright yellow "mirror" of passion fruit juice, giving the dessert an unsurpassable flair.

CRUST
1 cup all-purpose flour
1 ounce almonds, toasted (see Index) and chopped fine (about ¼ cup)
¼ teaspoon salt
6 tablespoons unsalted butter, chilled and cut into ½-inch pieces
1 large egg yolk, beaten
1 tablespoon cold water or more if necessary
¼ teaspoon almond extract
3 ounces high-quality imported white chocolate, chopped fine

MOUSSE
1½ teaspoons unflavored gelatin
2 tablespoons passion fruit liqueur, such as La Grande Passion
2 large eggs, separated, at room temperature
¼ cup granulated sugar
¼ cup strained fresh or bottled passion fruit juice
½ cup heavy (whipping) cream

MIRROR
¾ cup plus 2 tablespoons strained fresh or bottled passion fruit juice
2 tablespoons passion fruit liqueur, such as La Grande Passion
1¼ teaspoons unflavored gelatin

White chocolate leaves for garnish (see Index)

1. *Make the crust:* In a medium bowl, combine the flour, chopped almonds, and salt. Add the butter pieces. Using a pastry blender or two knives, cut in the butter until the mixture resembles coarse meal. In a small bowl, beat together the yolk, cold water, and almond extract. Tossing the flour-butter mixture with a fork, sprinkle it with the liquids, tossing just until moistened and the dough holds together when pinched between your thumb and

forefinger. (You may have to add more water, 1 tablespoon at a time.) Gather the dough into a thick disk and wrap it in wax paper. Refrigerate for at least 1 hour or overnight.

2. On a lightly floured work surface, roll the dough into a 12-inch circle. Ease the dough carefully into a 9-inch fluted tart pan with a removable bottom. Trim the overhanging dough, leaving a ¼-inch lip. Press the dough into the bottom of the pan, being careful not to leave any air bubbles. Press the dough up the sides of the pan so that it rises ¼ inch above the top edge of the pan. Prick the dough well with a fork. Line the dough with foil and chill for at least 30 minutes and up to 4 hours.

3. Position a rack in the center of the oven and preheat to 375°F. Weight the foil-lined dough with dry beans or rice. Bake until the dough is set, about 10 minutes. Remove the foil with the beans and continue baking until the shell is golden brown, 15–20 minutes longer, using a fork to pierce any air bubbles that appear in the crust during baking. Cool the pastry shell for 2 minutes, then sprinkle with the white chocolate. Let stand until chocolate is softened, about 5 minutes. Using the back of a spoon, spread the chocolate evenly on the bottom and sides of the shell. Cool the shell completely on a wire cake rack.

4. *Make the mousse:* In a small heatproof bowl, sprinkle the gelatin over the liqueur and let stand until softened, about 5 minutes. Place the bowl in a medium saucepan and add enough water to the saucepan to come halfway up the sides of the bowl. Bring the water to a simmer over medium heat and cook, stirring the gelatin mixture constantly until dissolved, about 3 minutes. Remove from the heat and let the gelatin mixture stand in the hot water.

5. In a medium bowl, using a hand-held electric mixer set at high speed, beat the egg yolks and sugar until thickened and doubled in volume, about 2 minutes. Beat in the passion fruit juice. Beat in the gelatin mixture.

6. In a medium-size grease-free bowl, with clean, dry beaters, beat the egg whites just until soft peaks form. Using a rubber spatula, fold the whites into the passion fruit mixture.

7. In a chilled medium bowl, using a hand-held mixer set at high speed, whip the heavy cream just until soft peaks form and fold it into the passion fruit mixture. Spread the mousse evenly in the bottom of the cooled pastry shell. Cover loosely with plastic wrap and refrigerate until the mousse is set, about 3 hours.

8. *Make the mirror:* In a small saucepan, combine the passion fruit juice and liqueur. Sprinkle the gelatin over the liquids and let stand until softened, about 5 minutes. Heat the mixture over very low heat, stirring constantly, until the gelatin is dissolved, about 3 minutes. Transfer the mixture to a medium bowl set in a larger bowl of ice water. Cool the mixture, stirring often, until syrupy, about 5 minutes.

9. Carefully pour the gelatin mixture over the set mousse, tilting and rotating the tart to spread the "mirror" evenly over the surface of the mousse. Refrigerate until the mirror is set, about 15 minutes. (The tart can be prepared and refrigerated up to 1 day ahead. Don't cover with plastic wrap, which could easily adhere to the passion fruit mirror. If you have a large plastic "pie saver" with a snap-on cover, this is the perfect opportunity to use it.) Just before serving, remove the sides of the pan. Garnish the tart with white chocolate leaves arranged in a spoke pattern.

Makes 6–8 servings

Chocolate Morsels: Fresh passion fruit can be found every now and then at varying prices throughout the year. Wrinkled skin is a sign of ripeness, so don't pass over these fruits. To use, cut the fruits in half. Using a teaspoon, scoop the pulp out into a wire strainer set over a bowl. Rub the pulp through the strainer with a wooden spoon, discarding the seeds left in the strainer. Unfortunately, you'll get only about 1 tablespoon juice from each fruit. (Since this recipe calls for 18 tablespoons of strained juice, you'd need 18 passion fruits.) An excellent substitute is bottled passion fruit juice, blended with white grape juice and found at many health food stores.

To keep a crisp crust from getting soggy when topped with a moist filling, use the trick described in this recipe: Sprinkle chopped chocolate over the hot pastry shell and then spread the melted chocolate evenly in the crust, using the back of a spoon. Use bittersweet, milk, or white chocolate to complement the flavor of your filling.

Berry and Chocolate Sandwich

Quick and elegant, this gorgeous "sandwich" is a close relative to a shortcake. During the summer I toast the pound cake slices right on the grill, estimating about 3 minutes per side over medium coals. If you've cooked a main course on the grill, be sure to scrape the grill rack clean before toasting the pound cake.

1 pint fresh strawberries, hulled
  and sliced
1 cup fresh raspberries
⅓ cup granulated sugar
¾ cup heavy (whipping) cream
2 tablespoons unsalted butter
6 ounces bittersweet chocolate,
  chopped fine
1 loaf-shaped pound cake,
  preferably homemade, cut into
  12 ⅜-inch-thick slices
4 whole strawberries for garnish
  (optional)

1. In a medium bowl, lightly toss together the strawberries, raspberries, and sugar to mix. Cover and refrigerate until the berries give off some juices, at least 4 hours or overnight.

2. In a small saucepan over low heat, bring the cream and butter to a low simmer. Remove the pan from the heat and add the chocolate. Let stand for 5 minutes to melt the chocolate, then whisk until smooth. (The chocolate sauce can be made up to 2 days ahead, covered, and refrigerated. Reheat in the top part of a double boiler over hot water.)

3. Position the broiler rack about 4 inches from the source of heat and preheat the broiler. Toast the pound cake slices until lightly browned on both sides, turning once, 2–3 minutes altogether.

4. If necessary, warm the chocolate sauce. Divide the sauce evenly among six dessert plates, pouring it directly onto the plates. Tilt the plates so the sauce covers the bottoms of the plates. Make six sandwiches: Place one slice of cake on each plate and drizzle with half of the berry juices. With a slotted spoon, spoon the berries evenly over the slices. Top with the remaining pound cake slices and drizzle the slices with the berry juices left in the bowl. If desired, with a small sharp knife, leaving the stems attached, slice the 4 whole strawberries and slightly spread each slice to form a fan. Place a strawberry fan on top of each sandwich and serve immediately.

Makes 6 servings

Raspberry-Topped Fudge Tart

What a knockout! There's something strikingly dramatic about the color combination of luscious red raspberries nested on top of a midnight-dark, fudgy filling. The buttery crust, which melts in your mouth, is quickly mixed in the food processor and then simply pressed into the pan, eliminating the sticky problem of rolling out such a rich, sweet dough.

DOUGH:
1 cup all-purpose flour
6 tablespoons (¾ stick) unsalted
    butter, chilled and cut into 6
    pieces
3 tablespoons granulated sugar
¼ teaspoon salt
1 large egg yolk, lightly beaten

FILLING:
1½ cups heavy (whipping) cream
9 ounces bittersweet chocolate,
    chopped fine
3 tablespoons unsalted butter, at
    room temperature
2 tablespoons light corn syrup

½ cup red currant jelly
3 cups fresh raspberries

1. *Make the crust:* Position a rack in the center of the oven and preheat to 375°F. In a food processor fitted with the metal blade, combine the flour, butter, sugar, and salt and pulse 15–20 times, until the mixture resembles fine crumbs. With the machine running, add the egg yolk and process just until the dough is moistened. Do not overprocess the dough. Gather up into a thick disk. Press the dough evenly in the bottom and up the sides of a 9-inch round tart pan with a removable bottom. Using a fork, prick the dough well.

2. Bake the tart shell until golden brown, 15–20 minutes, using a fork to pierce any air bubbles that appear during baking. Cool the shell completely on a wire cake rack.

3. *Make the filling:* In a medium saucepan over medium heat, bring the heavy cream just to a low simmer. Remove the pan from the heat and add the chocolate, butter, and corn syrup. Let the mixture stand until the chocolate is melted, about 3 minutes, then whisk until smooth. Pour the fudge filling into the cooled tart shell. Cover loosely with plastic wrap and refrigerate until the filling is firm, about 2 hours.

4. *Assemble the tart:* In a small saucepan, heat the jelly over low heat, stirring often, until melted and smooth; cool slightly.

5. Arrange the raspberries, rounded sides up, in concentric circles on the surface of the filling. Using a pastry brush, glaze the berries with the melted jelly. Chill for 5 minutes to set the glaze. (The tart can be prepared up to 1 day ahead, covered loosely with plastic wrap, and refrigerated.)

Makes 6–8 servings

Chocolate Morsels: You can substitute 2 pints fresh strawberries for the raspberries. Rinse the strawberries quickly and pat dry with paper towels. Hull the strawberries and cut them lengthwise into $\frac{1}{8}$-inch-thick slices. Arrange overlapping strawberry slices in concentric circles over the filling and glaze with the melted currant jelly.

San Andreas Fudge Torte

San Andreas Fudge Torte gets its name from the fissured top crust that develops during baking. The crunchy layer provides textural contrast to the unctuous chocolate layer below. You must serve this flourless delicacy chilled with a big dollop of whipped cream to balance the richness. Some fresh berries are perfect with this too.

12 tablespoons (1½ sticks) unsalted
  butter, cut into pieces
5 ounces semisweet chocolate,
  chopped fine
3 ounces unsweetened chocolate,
  chopped fine
½ cup strong brewed coffee
4 large eggs, at room temperature
1 cup granulated sugar
1 cup heavy (whipping) cream
2 tablespoons confectioners' sugar

1. Position a rack in the center of the oven and preheat to 350°F. Lightly butter the bottom and sides of an 8-inch round springform pan.

2. In a medium saucepan, melt the butter over medium-low heat. Remove from the heat and add the chopped chocolates and coffee. Let stand until the chocolate melts, about 3 minutes. Whisk until smooth.

3. In a large heatproof bowl, whisk the eggs and sugar until blended. Set the bowl over a medium saucepan of hot, not simmering, water. (The bottom of the bowl must touch the water.) Continue whisking until the sugar is dissolved and the mixture is hot to the touch (110–120°F), about 3 minutes. Remove the bowl from the water.

4. Using a hand-held electric mixer set at high speed, beat the hot egg mixture until it is pale yellow and has tripled in volume, about 5 minutes.

5. Stir about one-fourth of the egg mixture into the chocolate mixture to lighten it. Using a rubber spatula, fold in the remaining egg mixture. Transfer the batter to the prepared pan and spread it evenly, smoothing the top.

6. Bake until a toothpick inserted in the center of the torte comes out with a moist crumb, 35–40 minutes. Run a sharp knife around the inside edge of the torte to loosen it from the sides of the pan. Let it cool completely on a wire cake rack. (The torte will fall during cooling.) Cover the cake with plastic wrap and refrigerate until chilled, at least 2 hours or overnight.

7. In a chilled medium bowl, beat the heavy cream just until soft peaks form. Beat in the confectioners' sugar.

8. Release the sides of the springform pan. Slice the torte using a large sharp knife dipped in hot water and wiped dry between the cuts. Top each serving with a dollop of whipped cream.

Makes 8 servings

Irish Cream–Chip Cheesecake

Adults only for this hedonistic, one-of-a-kind cheesecake. I developed this heady recipe for a St. Patrick's Day celebration, but the result was so impressive that I serve it year-round.

1¾ cups (about 7 ounces) finely
   crushed chocolate wafer cookies
6 tablespoons (¾ stick) unsalted
   butter, melted
2 pounds cream cheese, softened
1 cup granulated sugar
3 large eggs, at room temperature
2 large egg yolks, at room
   temperature
1 cup sour cream, at room
   temperature
1 cup Irish whiskey cream
   liqueur, such as Bailey's Irish
   Cream
1 cup miniature semisweet
   chocolate chips, divided

1. Position a rack in the center of the oven and preheat to 350°F. Lightly butter the bottom and sides of a 10-inch round springform pan. Tightly wrap the outside bottom of the pan with aluminum foil.

2. In a medium bowl, combine the chocolate wafer crumbs and melted butter. Press the mixture evenly into the bottom of the pan, making sure the crust extends 1 inch up the sides.

3. In a large bowl, using a hand-held electric mixer set at medium-high speed, beat the cream cheese and sugar until smooth, about 2 minutes. One at a time, beat in the eggs and yolks, scraping the bottom and sides of the bowl often with a rubber spatula. Beat in the sour cream and liqueur. Stir in ¾ cup

of the chocolate chips. Pour the cheesecake batter into the prepared pan and sprinkle the top with the remaining ¼ cup chips.

4. Bake until the edges of the cheesecake have risen and are beginning to brown, 60–75 minutes. Run a sharp knife around the inside of the pan to release the cheesecake from the sides of the pan. Cool the cheesecake completely on a wire cake rack.

5. Release the sides of the springform pan and wrap the cheesecake in plastic wrap. Refrigerate until well chilled, at least 2 hours or overnight. Slice the cheesecake using a large sharp knife dipped in hot water and wiped dry between cuts. (The cheesecake can be prepared up to 3 days ahead, covered, and refrigerated.)

Makes 10–12 servings

9
At the Soda Fountain

Homemade Chocolate Syrup
Gold Rush Sundae
Chocolate Malteds in Chocolate Bags
Chocolate Fiesta Cake
Golden Gate Ice-Cream Pie
Blum's Coffee Crunch
Strawberry Fudge Ripple Ice Cream
Black and White Soda
Chocolate Banana Cream Pudding
Parker House Cream Pie
North Beach Chocolate Sauce
Schrafft's Famous Hot Fudge Sauce
Chocolate Peppermint Chip Ice Cream
Chocolate Truffle–Vanilla Bean Ice Cream

Homemade Chocolate Syrup

Dedicated chocophiles will want to have a jar of this versatile sauce tucked into the refrigerator to come to the rescue when nothing but a little chocolate will do the trick. Stir a couple of tablespoons into milk (hot or cold). Or drizzle it onto desserts and ice cream. In cases of dire need, lick it off your finger (or a friend's!). Packed into attractive pint jars, it is the perfect homemade gift for the chocolate lover in your life.

1½ cups granulated sugar
¾ cup nonalkalized cocoa powder,
   such as Hershey's
⅛ teaspoon salt
1 cup hot water
2 teaspoons vanilla extract

1. In a medium-size heavy saucepan, whisk together the sugar, cocoa, and salt. Gradually whisk in the hot water until smooth. Bring to a boil over medium heat. Whisking constantly, cook for 3 minutes. Remove the pan from the heat and stir in the vanilla.

2. Pour the syrup into a clean container and cool completely. (The syrup will keep for up to 1 week, covered tightly and stored in the refrigerator.)

Makes 2 cups

Gold Rush Sundae

❧

I served a similar sundae at Blum's marble soda fountain counter. Mounds of luscious vanilla ice cream, smothered with a hot mocha sauce, then covered with heaps of crushed gold coffee crunch—irresistible.

½ cup heavy (whipping) cream
1 tablespoon confectioners' sugar
1 quart vanilla ice cream
1⅓ cups North Beach Chocolate
    Sauce (see Index), warmed
½ recipe Blum's Coffee Crunch
    (see Index)
2 ounces pecans, toasted (see
    Index) and chopped coarse
    (about ½ cup)

1. In a chilled medium bowl, using a hand-held electric mixer set at high speed, beat the cream with the confectioners' sugar until soft peaks form. Refrigerate the whipped cream until ready to serve.

2. Divide scoops of the ice cream evenly among four large dessert bowls or goblets. Divide the warm sauce evenly over the ice cream. Sprinkle with the crunch and the nuts. Top each with a dollop of whipped cream and serve immediately.

Makes 4 servings

Chocolate Malteds in Chocolate Bags

❧

Without a doubt, this is the classiest way to serve that frosty favorite, the chocolate malted. Many restaurants create these elaborate chocolate bags to hold other desserts, like mousses, ice cream sundaes, or fruits. You'll think of inventive ways to use them too.

BAGS
4 small paper bags (3 inches tall
    with 4″ × 2″ bases) that are
    lined with a coated surface (see
    Note)
1¾ pounds bittersweet chocolate,
    chopped very fine

MALTEDS
2½ cups vanilla ice cream
⅔ cup Homemade Chocolate
    Syrup (see Index)
1 cup cold milk
¼–½ cup malt powder, to taste

Note: Laminated bags used for fresh coffee beans are perfect. Purchase new bags from your coffee purveyor. Using pinking shears, cut the bags to a 3-inch height. If necessary, substitute brown paper lunch bags. Brush the bags lightly with vegetable oil. The bags will soak up the oil.

1. *Make the bags:* In the top part of a double boiler over hot, not simmering, water, heat the chocolate, stirring often, until almost melted. Remove the top part of the double boiler from the bottom and let the chocolate stand, stirring often, until completely melted. Keep the melted chocolate warm on a heating pad set at low. Cover the pad with plastic wrap to protect from spills.

2. Place the opened paper bags on a baking sheet. Pour about ¼ cup of the melted chocolate into a bag. Using a small pastry brush, paint the chocolate

up the inside of the bag to coat evenly. Repeat the procedure with the other bags. Refrigerate the bags until the chocolate is firm, 10–15 minutes. Pour another 3 tablespoons melted chocolate into the bag and coat a second time, making sure to apply extra to the bottom and corners of the bags. Refrigerate again until the chocolate is firm, about 15 minutes.

3. Remove a bag from the refrigerator. Carefully peel away the paper bag. Using the reserved melted chocolate, patch any areas that may need attention. Return the chocolate bag to the refrigerator for 10 minutes, until completely set. Repeat with the other bags. Store the chocolate bags in the refrigerator until ready to use.

4. *Make the chocolate malteds:* In a blender, process the ice cream, Homemade Chocolate Syrup, milk, and malt powder until smooth. Pour the malteds into the bags and serve immediately with straws.

Makes 4 servings

Chocolate Fiesta Cake

Another Golden Gate great. At Blum's the cake was lemon chiffon, but of course I prefer it with a chocolate angel food. It is swirled with loads of whipped cream, then encrusted with chunks of coffee crunch. The crunch has a tendency to "melt" when it comes in contact with the whipped cream for too long, so decorate the cake only a few hours before serving.

COCOA ANGEL FOOD CAKE
1¼ cups superfine sugar, divided
¾ cup cake flour
¼ cup Dutch-process cocoa powder, such as Droste
12 large egg whites, at room temperature
1 teaspoon cream of tartar
¼ teaspoon salt
1 teaspoon vanilla extract

CREAM FROSTING
2 cups heavy (whipping) cream
¼ cup confectioners' sugar
1 teaspoon vanilla extract

Blum's Coffee Crunch, crushed coarse (see Index)

1. *Make the cake:* Position a rack in the center of the oven and preheat to 350°F. Do not butter or flour the tube pan. (Greasing the pan will inhibit the batter from clinging to the pan and rising properly.) Sift ¾ cup of the superfine sugar, the flour, and cocoa together through a wire strainer onto a sheet of wax paper.

2. In a large grease-free bowl, using a hand-held electric mixer set at low speed, with clean, dry beaters, beat the egg whites until very foamy, about 30 seconds. Add the cream of tartar and salt. Increase the speed to medium-high and continue beating, gradually adding the remaining ½ cup superfine sugar, just until the whites form stiff peaks. Do not overbeat the whites. Add the vanilla extract, but do not stir it in.

3. One-third at a time, resift the flour mixture over the beaten whites and fold together, using a balloon whisk or a rubber spatula. Transfer the batter to a 10-inch round tube pan and smooth the top evenly with a rubber spatula.

142

4. Bake for about 60 minutes, until the cake has risen and a long bamboo skewer inserted in the center of the cake comes out clean. Completely cool the cake upside down. The cake must clear the counter. Balance the edges of the pan on three equally spaced coffee mugs if necessary. Cooling will take at least 4 hours or overnight. (The cake can be prepared up to 3 days ahead, wrapped tightly in plastic wrap, and stored at room temperature.)

5. *Make the frosting:* In a large chilled bowl, using a hand-held electric mixer set at high speed, beat together the cream and confectioners' sugar just until stiff. Beat in the vanilla.

6. *Assemble the cake:* Using a serrated knife, cut the cake in half horizontally. Place the bottom layer on a serving platter. Using a metal cake spatula, spread the layer with about ½ cup of the whipped cream, then top with the second layer. Frost the top and sides of the cake with the remaining whipped cream.

7. No more than 4 hours before serving, press the crushed coffee crunch onto the whipped cream frosting. (The cake can be prepared up to 6 hours ahead, and refrigerated, uncovered.) Use a serrated knife to cut the cake into wedges.

Makes 8–10 servings

Golden Gate Ice-Cream Pie

A thick slab of ice-cold ice-cream pie is sure to hit the spot, especially on a hot summer day. Back this up with a tall, frosted glass of seltzer to make it an authentic soda fountain snack.

1⅓ cups (about 6 ounces) crushed
    chocolate wafer cookies
4 tablespoons (½ stick) unsalted
    butter, melted
1 quart vanilla ice cream, slightly
    softened
2 cups Homemade Chocolate
    Syrup (see Index), divided
1 quart chocolate ice cream,
    slightly softened
½ recipe Blum's Coffee Crunch
    (see Index)

1. In a medium bowl, combine the cookie crumbs and melted butter. Press the mixture firmly and evenly into a lightly buttered 9-inch pie pan. Place the crust in the freezer until firm, about 15 minutes.

2. Spread the crust evenly with the vanilla ice cream. Drizzle ⅔ cup of the chocolate syrup over the ice cream. Spread the chocolate ice cream over the vanilla-syrup layer, mounding the ice cream into a dome. Cover the pie with plastic wrap and place in the freezer until firm, at least 2 hours.

3. Press the coffee crunch over the top of the pie. Using a sharp knife dipped in hot water between slices, cut the pie into wedges. Serve each piece drizzled with some of the remaining chocolate syrup.

Makes 8 servings

Blum's Coffee Crunch

Even though I was only 19 years old when I worked at Blum's, I knew a good thing when I ate it! With an intriguing, foamy texture and a deep blond color, Blum's famous Coffee Crunch was used in a parade of its best desserts. I begged one of the bakers for the recipe. She divulged the "top secret formula," with threats of death if I ever shared it. I found out later that she had repeated the recipe (and threats) to an enormous number of curious cooks, including the food section of a San Francisco newspaper. Secret or not, it is fabulous.

1½ cups granulated sugar
¼ cup strong brewed coffee
¼ cup light corn syrup
1 tablespoon baking soda

1. Lightly oil a large baking sheet. Attach a candy thermometer to a tall saucepan of at least 4-quart capacity, because the crunch will foam up in the pan and could boil over. Make sure the end of the thermometer does not touch the bottom of the pan.

2. Combine the sugar, coffee, and corn syrup in the pan. Bring to a boil over medium-high heat, stirring constantly to help dissolve the sugar. Stop stirring and boil until the thermometer reads 300°F. Remove the pan from the heat and sift the baking soda into the mixture. (The sifting is important, or you will have undissolved nuggets of soda in your crunch.) Using a wooden spoon, stir the crunch briefly, just to incorporate the soda. Be careful—it will foam up to about four times its volume.

3. Pour the mixture out onto the baking sheet. Cool completely. Break the crunch into pieces of desired size. (The crunch can be made up to 4 weeks ahead and stored in an airtight container at room temperature.)

Makes about 3 cups crushed

Chocolate Morsels: This recipe halves easily, but use a 2-quart saucepan so the syrup doesn't boil over.

Strawberry Fudge Ripple Ice Cream

My poor little ice-cream maker hardly gets a break all summer long! I love to treat my guests to homemade ice cream. This fruity specialty makes an appearance at the height of strawberry season, hedonistically woven with frozen ribbons of chewy chocolate fudge.

1 pint fresh strawberries, hulled
    and chopped coarse
1 cup superfine sugar, divided
5 large egg yolks, at room
    temperature
1 cup heavy (whipping) cream
1 cup milk
1 teaspoon vanilla extract
⅔ cup Schrafft's Famous Hot
    Fudge Sauce (see Index),
    warmed

1. In a medium bowl, combine the strawberries and ½ cup of the sugar. Cover and refrigerate until the strawberries give off their juices, at least 2 hours or overnight. Drain the strawberries, reserving the juices.

2. In a food processor fitted with the metal blade or a blender, puree half of the chopped strawberries and the reserved juices.

3. In a medium bowl, whisk together the egg yolks and the remaining ½ cup sugar. In a heavy-bottomed medium saucepan, bring the cream and the milk to a simmer over low heat. Gradually whisk the hot liquids into the yolk mixture. Rinse out the saucepan and return the mixture to it. Using a wooden spoon, stir the cream mixture constantly over medium-low heat until thick enough to lightly coat the back of the spoon. (An instant-read thermometer inserted into the mixture will read about 175°F.)

4. Remove the pan from the heat and strain into a medium bowl placed in a larger bowl of ice water. Let stand, stirring often, until the custard is very cold, about 15 minutes. Remove the bowl from the water and stir in the chopped strawberries, strawberry puree, and vanilla. (The custard can be prepared up to 1 day ahead, covered tightly with plastic wrap, and refrigerated.)

5. Pour the strawberry custard into the container of an ice-cream maker and freeze according to the manufacturer's instructions. Transfer the ice cream to an airtight container. Stir in the warm fudge sauce. Freeze for at least 4 hours or overnight.

Makes about 1 quart

Black and White Soda

After making thousands of ice cream sodas in my day, my mouth still waters at the thought of one of these foamy chocolate/vanilla drinks. For the ultimate soda, use seltzer from a home dispenser fitted with the carbon dioxide cylinders, available at houseware stores.

2 tablespoons Homemade
  Chocolate Syrup (see Index)
1 big scoop plus 2 tablespoons
  vanilla ice cream
1 cup seltzer or club soda

1. In a chilled tall glass, using a long spoon, stir together the chocolate syrup and about 2 tablespoons of the ice cream until the ice cream melts slightly.

2. Pour (or squirt) the seltzer into the glass, stopping 1 inch from the top of the glass. Perch the ice cream on the lip of the glass so half of it touches the soda and foams but the other half is hanging over the edge. Serve immediately with a long straw and a long spoon.

Makes 1 serving

Chocolate Banana Cream Pudding

Whenever I visit the South, I make a beeline to the nearest luncheonette and order a dish of meringue-topped banana and vanilla wafer pudding. I've given it a new dimension with the addition of chocolate.

2 tablespoons cornstarch
3 cups milk, divided
1⅔ cups granulated sugar, divided
3 large eggs, separated, at room temperature
1 large egg yolk, at room temperature

3 ounces semisweet chocolate, chopped fine
1 teaspoon vanilla extract
1 12-ounce box vanilla wafers
5 medium bananas, sliced into ½-inch-thick rounds
⅛ teaspoon cream of tartar

1. Position a rack in the top third of the oven and preheat to 350°F. In a heavy-bottomed medium saucepan, whisk together the cornstarch and 2 tablespoons of the milk until smooth. Whisk in the remaining milk, 1 cup of the sugar, and the egg yolks. Stirring constantly with a wooden spoon, cook over medium-low heat until the custard is thick enough to coat the spoon, about 6 minutes. (An instant-read thermometer inserted in the custard will read about 175°F.) Do not let the custard boil. Remove from the heat, add the chocolate and vanilla, and whisk until the chocolate is melted.

2. Spread half of the vanilla wafers in the bottom of a 9″ × 13″ baking pan. Arrange the bananas over the wafers and top with the remaining wafers. Pour the chocolate custard evenly into the pan.

3. In a medium-size grease-free bowl, using a hand-held electric mixer set at low speed, with clean, dry beaters, beat the egg whites until foamy. Add cream of tartar, increase the speed to high, and beat just until the egg whites form soft peaks. Still beating, gradually add the remaining ⅔ cup sugar and beat until the whites form stiff, shiny peaks. Using a metal cake spatula, swirl the meringue over the pudding, so that it touches the sides of the pan.

4. Bake until the meringue is lightly browned, 10–15 minutes. Refrigerate the pudding until well chilled, at least 4 hours or overnight. (The pudding can be prepared up to 2 days ahead and refrigerated, uncovered.)

Makes 12 servings

Parker House Cream Pie

ৰ৺ৡ

Why do we call this dessert, so obviously a cake, a pie? In Early American cooking terminology, anything that was cooked in a round dish could be called a "pie." Without its chocolate cap this is called Boston cream pie. To accent the chocolate further, I've added miniature chocolate chips to the custard filling. I like it as a summer dessert and serve it with sliced apricots and berries.

CAKE
¾ cup all-purpose flour
¼ teaspoon salt
4 large eggs, separated, at room
  temperature
¾ cup granulated sugar, divided
¾ teaspoon vanilla extract
⅛ teaspoon cream of tartar

FILLING
3 tablespoons cornstarch
1½ cups milk, divided
6 tablespoons granulated sugar
5 large egg yolks, at room
  temperature
2 tablespoons unsalted butter, cut
  into pieces
¾ teaspoon vanilla extract
½ cup miniature semisweet
  chocolate chips

ICING
6 tablespoons heavy (whipping)
  cream
2 ounces semisweet chocolate,
  chopped fine
½ cup confectioners' sugar, sifted

1. *Make the cake:* Position a rack in the center of the oven and preheat to 350°F. Lightly butter the bottom only of a 9-inch springform pan. Line the bottom of the pan with a round of wax paper. Sift the flour and salt together through a wire strainer onto a piece of wax paper.

2. In a large bowl, using a hand-held electric mixer set at high speed, beat the egg yolks with 6 tablespoons of the sugar until the mixture is pale yellow and forms a thick ribbon when the beaters are lifted, about 3 minutes. Beat in the vanilla.

3. In a large grease-free bowl, using a hand-held electric mixer set at low speed, with clean, dry beaters, beat the egg whites until foamy. Add the cream of tartar, increase the speed to high, and beat just until soft peaks begin to form. Still beating, gradually add the remaining 6 tablespoons sugar and beat until the egg whites form stiff, shiny peaks. Stir about one-fourth of the egg whites into the yolk mixture to lighten it. Pour the lightened yolk mixture on top of the remaining whites. Sift half of the flour mixture over the egg mixture. Using a large balloon whisk or a rubber spatula, fold the flour and egg mixture together. (Some traces of whites will remain.) Sift the remaining flour mixture over the batter and fold together until blended. Scrape the batter into the prepared pan, smoothing the top with the spatula.

4. Bake until the top of the cake springs back when pressed lightly in the center, 25–30 minutes. Transfer the cake to a wire cake rack and cool for 10 minutes. Run a sharp knife around the edges of the cake to loosen it from the sides of the pan. Invert the cake onto a wire cake rack and carefully peel off the wax paper. Turn the cake right side up and cool completely.

5. *Make the filling:* In a heavy-bottomed medium saucepan, whisk the cornstarch with ¼ cup of the milk until smooth. Whisk in the sugar, egg yolks, and remaining 1¼ cups milk. Bring the mixture to a simmer over medium heat, stirring constantly with a wooden spoon. Remove the pan from the heat and stir in the butter and vanilla. Press a sheet of plastic wrap directly onto the surface of the custard. Using a sharp knife, cut a few slits in the wrap to allow the steam to escape. Let the custard cool completely, then refrigerate until chilled, about 2 hours. Stir in the chocolate chips.

6. *Make the icing:* In a small saucepan, bring the cream to a low simmer over medium heat. Remove the pan from the heat, add the chocolate, and let stand until the chocolate is softened, about 3 minutes. Add the confectioners' sugar and whisk until smooth. Let the icing cool until tepid but pourable.

7. *Assemble the cake:* Using a serrated knife, cut the cake horizontally into two equal layers. Spread the bottom layer with the custard. Top with the second cake layer. Evenly frost the top of the cake with the icing. Refrigerate until the icing is set, about 15 minutes. (The cake can be prepared up to 1 day ahead, covered with plastic wrap, and refrigerated.)

Makes 6–8 servings

North Beach Chocolate Sauce

The Italian-Americans in San Francisco's North Beach love their hot chocolate spiked with espresso and brandy, not dissimilar to the city's famous Irish coffee. This is tempting warm and at room temperature.

⅓ cup heavy (whipping) cream
6 tablespoons (¾ stick) unsalted
    butter, cut into pieces
1½ teaspoons instant espresso
    powder
8 ounces semisweet chocolate,
    chopped fine
2 tablespoons light corn syrup
2 tablespoons brandy

1. In a medium-size heavy saucepan over medium-low heat, bring the cream and butter to a low simmer. Remove the pan from the heat and whisk in the espresso powder until dissolved. Add the chocolate and let stand until the chocolate is softened, about 3 minutes. Whisk until smooth. Whisk in the corn syrup and brandy. Serve the sauce warm or at room temperature. (The sauce can be made up to 5 days ahead, covered tightly, and refrigerated. Reheat the sauce gently in the top of a double boiler if desired.)

Makes about 1½ cups

Schrafft's Famous Hot Fudge Sauce

Schrafft's, the late, lamented Olympus of New York soda fountains, was particularly well known for the quality of its hot fudge sauce. Fifteen years after it closed its last restaurant in 1973, Schrafft's happily reappeared as an ice-cream company. To celebrate its return, Schrafft's asked me to reformulate its original hot fudge recipe for the home cook. It took me a few tries, as the recipe made 150 quarts, but I finally got it right. It pours onto ice cream hot and molten but cools to a firm, chewy consistency. Simply put, this is the Great Hot Fudge Sauce of All Time.

1 cup granulated sugar
1 tablespoon nonalkalized cocoa
  powder, such as Hershey's
¾ cup heavy (whipping) cream,
  divided
¼ cup light corn syrup

2 tablespoons unsalted butter
2 ounces unsweetened chocolate,
  chopped fine
Few drops of malt vinegar
Pinch of salt
1 teaspoon vanilla extract

1. Attach a candy thermometer to a heavy-bottomed medium saucepan, making sure it doesn't touch the bottom of the pan. Add the sugar and cocoa and whisk together. Gradually whisk in ¼ cup of the cream until smooth.

2. Whisk in the remaining ½ cup cream, the corn syrup, butter, chocolate, vinegar, and salt. Bring to a boil over high heat, stirring constantly to dissolve sugar. When the mixture comes to a boil, stop stirring and reduce heat to medium-high. Cook until the candy thermometer reads 236°F, about 3 minutes. Remove the saucepan from the heat and stir in the vanilla. Let the sauce stand for about 10 minutes before serving. (The sauce can be prepared up to 1 week ahead, cooled, covered, and refrigerated. Reheat it slowly in the top part of a double boiler over simmering water, stirring often, before serving.)

Makes about 2 cups

Chocolate Morsels: The malt vinegar and corn syrup discourage sugar crystals from forming in the fudge sauce. You may substitute lemon juice or cider vinegar for the malt vinegar if you wish.

Chocolate Peppermint Chip Ice Cream

An overabundant crop of mint, like zucchini, can drive a gardener to distraction. Every summer my patience and imagination are taxed to the limit as I strive to use my burgeoning peppermint before it takes over the whole herb garden. Happily, chocolate and mint are a spirited combination, and after you've made this exceptional ice cream you'll be glad you planted that mint after all.

3 cups half-and-half
1 cup packed fresh whole
   peppermint leaves
6 large egg yolks
¾ cup granulated sugar
3 tablespoons Dutch-process cocoa
   powder, such as Droste
6 ounces bittersweet chocolate,
   chopped fine
½ cup semisweet chocolate chips

1. In a medium-size heavy nonaluminum saucepan, bring the half-and-half and mint to a low simmer over medium-low heat. Remove the pan from the heat, cover tightly, and let stand for 30 minutes to steep. Strain the mixture through a wire strainer into a medium bowl. Rinse out the saucepan.

2. In another medium bowl, whisk together the egg yolks, sugar, and cocoa until smooth. Gradually whisk in the half-and-half mixture. Return the mixture to the saucepan. Cook over medium-low heat, stirring constantly with a wooden spoon, until the custard has thickened enough to coat the back of the spoon, 3–4 minutes. Do not let the custard boil. (An instant-read thermometer will read about 175°F.) Strain the mixture through a wire strainer back into the medium bowl. Add the chopped chocolate, let stand for 1 minute, and then whisk until smooth. Place the bowl in a larger bowl filled with ice water and stir the mixture occasionally for 15–20 minutes until cold.

3. Pour the mixture into the container of an ice-cream maker and freeze according to the manufacturer's directions. Remove the container from the machine and stir in the chocolate chips. Transfer the ice cream to an airtight container and freeze for at least 4 hours or overnight. Homemade ice cream is best when eaten within 24 hours.

Makes about 1 quart

Chocolate Morsels: Keep the peppermint leaves whole. Chopping them will release their green chlorophyll into the milk and give your ice cream a brown-green tint.

To make Chocolate–Grand Marnier Ice Cream, substitute the zest of 1 large orange (removed with a vegetable peeler) for the mint. Steep the zest in the half-and-half. Add ¼ cup Grand Marnier to the ice-cream mixture with the chopped chocolate.

To make French Chocolate Ice Cream, delete the mint. Bring the half-and-half just to a low simmer; do not let it stand for 30 minutes, but instead proceed with the recipe. Substitute a 3-ounce bar of bittersweet chocolate, chopped coarse, for the chocolate chips.

Chocolate Truffle–
Vanilla Bean Ice Cream

Here is the ultimate chocolate-chunk ice cream, a super sophisticated affair to be reserved for extraspecial occasions. You will need an ice-cream maker for this recipe, and I recommend buying one of the inexpensive electric models that use regular ice cubes and table salt. Once you own one and realize how easy it is to use, you'll churn out quart after quart of homemade ice cream and sorbets.

TRUFFLES
6 tablespoons (¾ stick) unsalted
   butter, cut into pieces
8 ounces bittersweet chocolate,
   chopped fine
⅓ cup orange marmalade,
   preferably bitter orange
2 tablespoons Grand Marnier or
   other orange-flavored liqueur
¼ cup Dutch-process cocoa
   powder, such as Droste, for
   coating

ICE CREAM
3 cups half-and-half
1 cup granulated sugar
2 vanilla beans, halved lengthwise
6 large egg yolks
Pinch of salt

1. *Make the truffles:* In the top part of a double boiler over hot, not simmering, water, melt the butter. Add the chocolate and melt, stirring occasionally, until smooth. Remove the top part of the double boiler from the water. Add the orange marmalade and Grand Marnier and whisk until smooth. Cover with plastic wrap and refrigerate until firm, about 4 hours or overnight. Or place the mixture in the freezer until firm, about 2 hours.

2. Place the cocoa powder in a medium bowl. Using a melon baller or a teaspoon, scoop about 1½ teaspoons of the chocolate mixture and roll it between your palms to form a small round truffle. Roll the truffle in the cocoa to coat and lay it on a wax paper-lined baking sheet. Repeat the procedure with the remaining truffles. Cover tightly with plastic wrap and refrigerate until

ready to use. (The truffles can be prepared up to 5 days ahead, stored in tightly closed plastic bags, and refrigerated. They can be frozen for up to 1 month, wrapped tightly in double plastic bags.)

3. *Make the ice cream:* In a medium saucepan, bring the half-and-half, sugar, and vanilla beans to a simmer over low heat, stirring often to dissolve the sugar. Remove from the heat and let stand, covered, for 30 minutes. Remove the vanilla beans from the half-and-half mixture. Using the tip of a small sharp knife, scrape the tiny beans from the pods into the cream mixture and discard the pods.

4. In a medium bowl, whisk the egg yolks and salt until lightly beaten. Gradually whisk in the warm half-and-half mixture. Rinse out the saucepan and return the mixture to it. Using a wooden spoon, stir the half-and-half mixture constantly over medium-low heat until thick enough to lightly coat the back of the spoon, 3–4 minutes. (An instant-read thermometer inserted in the mixture will read about 175°F.) Do not let the custard boil. Strain the mixture through a wire strainer into a medium bowl set in a larger bowl of ice water. Stirring often, let the custard cool completely, about 20 minutes.

5. Freeze the custard in an ice-cream maker according to the manufacturer's instructions. When the ice cream is nearly frozen, stir the chocolate truffles into the vanilla bean ice cream. Transfer the ice cream to an airtight container and freeze until firm, at least 4 hours or overnight. Homemade ice cream is best when eaten within 24 hours.

Makes about 1½ quarts

Chocolate Morsels: You may substitute 1½ teaspoons vanilla extract for the vanilla beans if you wish. Stir the vanilla into the cooled custard at the end of step 3.

Index

Alkalized (Dutch process) cocoa powder, 4
Almonds, toasted, 10
Amazing Cake. *See* Wicky Wacky Chocolate Cake
Angel Food Cake, Cocoa, 142–43
    with Strawberry Whip, 26–27

Bags, Chocolate, 140–41
Baking chocolate, about, 2
Banana
    Chocolate Cream Pudding, 149
    -Chocolate Loaf Cake, 38–39
Bar Cookies. *See also* Brownies
    Blondies with Chocolate Chunks, 52–53
    Diane's Triple-Layered Delights, 64–65
    Impossible Dream Bars, 66
    Texas Pecan and Chocolate Toffee, 58–59
Berry and Chocolate Sandwich, 128–29
"Binding" (of chocolate), 7–8
Bittersweet chocolate, 2
    glaze, 74–75
Bittersweet Lemon Tart, 112–13
Black and White Ice Cream Soda, 148
Black and White Layer Cake, 24–25
Black-Eyed Susans. *See* Kiss Kookies

Blondies with Chocolate Chunks, 52–53
"Blooming" (of chocolate), 8
Blum's Coffee Crunch, 145
Boston Cream Pie, 150–51
Bread Pudding, Chocolate-Raisin, 67
Breakfast. *See* Chocolate French Toast
Brown sugar, about, 11
Brownies. *See also* Bar Cookies
    Lois's, 54–55
    Peanut Butter and Milk Chocolate, 51
Bûche de Noël, 98–100
Buckeyes. *See* Kiss Kookies
Bundt Cake, Chocolate-Orange, 36–37
Butter, about, 9
Buttercream, 122–24
Buttermilk
    about, 11
    -Chocolate Snackin' Cake, 30–31
    substitution for, 11
Butterscotch Brownies (Blondies), 52–53

Cacao, 1–2
Cake, 15–39. *See also* Cheesecake; Genoise; Torte
    Banana-Chocolate Loaf, 38–39
    Berry and Chocolate Sandwich, 128–29
    Black and White Layer, 24–25

    Chocolate-Buttermilk, 30–31
    Chocolate Fiesta, 142–43
    Chocolate Mayonnaise, 20–21
    Chocolate-Orange Bundt, 36–37
    Chocolate Pound, 22–23
    Chocolate Zucchini, 28–29
    Cocoa Angel Food, 142–43
    with Strawberry Whip, 26–27
    Double Chocolate–Sour Cream Layer, 16–17
    garnishes for, 14
    German Chocolate, 18–19
    Mississippi Mud, 70–71
    Parker House Cream Pie, 150–51
    Rigo Jansci, 95–97
    Sachertorte, 78–79
    Swiss Truffle Loaf, 92–94
    Tiramisù, 108–9
    White Chocolate Celebration, 122–24
    White Chocolate–Pistachio Tea Bread, 117–19
    Wicky Wacky Chocolate, 34–35
Cake flour, about, 10
Cakey Chocolate Chip–Raisin Cookies, 60–61
Camellia leaves (chocolate), 14
Cashews, unsalted, 10
Cheese filling (for Tiramisù), 108–9

Cheesecake
  Chocolate Cranberry, 74–75
  Chocolate Swirl, with
    Chocolate-Nut Crust,
    72–73
  Irish Cream-Chip, 134–35
Chewy Chocolate and White
    Chocolate Chip Cookies,
    62–63
Chocolate. *See also* specific
    recipes
  about, 1–8
  chips, 4
  chopping, 7
  curls, making, 13
  "flavored" products, 5
  leaves, 14
  liquor, 1–2
  making, 1–2
  melting, 7–8
  storing, 8
Chocolate and Berry Sandwich,
    128–29
Chocolate Angel Food Cake,
    26–27
Chocolate Bags, 140–41
Chocolate Banana Cream
    Pudding, 149
Chocolate-Banana Loaf Cake,
    38–39
Chocolate Bûche de Noël,
    98–100
Chocolate-Buttermilk Snackin'
    Cake, 30–31
Chocolate Cashew Tart. *See*
    Chocolate Walnut Tart
Chocolate Chip Peppermint Ice
    Cream, 154–55
Chocolate Chip-Raisin Cookies,
    Cakey, 60–61
Chocolate Cookies, Chewy, with
    White Chocolate Chips,
    62–63
Chocolate Cranberry
    Cheesecake, 74–75
Chocolate-Dipped Orange
    Cookies, 106–7

Chocolate Fiesta Cake, 142–43
Chocolate Fondue, Tropical,
    with Seasonal Fruits, 102
Chocolate French Toast, 103
Chocolate Fudge
  Nut, 45
  Classic, 44–45
  Flavored, 45
  Make-it-Easy, 42–43
Chocolate Malteds in Chocolate
    Bags, 140–41
Chocolate Mayonnaise Cake
    with Easy Cocoa Frosting,
    20–21
Chocolate-Orange Bundt Cake,
    36–37
Chocolate Orange Mousse Pie,
    120–21
Chocolate-Peanut Butter
    Meltaways, 48–49
Chocolate Peanut Pie, 68–69
Chocolate Pecan Toffee Cookies,
    58–59
Chocolate Peppermint Chip Ice
    Cream, 154–55
Chocolate Pound Cake, 22–23
Chocolate-Raisin Bread
    Pudding, , 67
Chocolate Raspberry Trifle,
    84–85
Chocolate Roll. *See* Bûche de
    Noël
Chocolate Sauce, North Beach,
    152. *See also* Chocolate
    Syrup; Hot Fudge Sauce
Chocolate-Sour Cream Layer
    Cake, 16–17
Chocolate Swirl Cheesecake with
    Chocolate-Nut Crust, 72–73
Chocolate Syrup, 86–87, 138.
    See also Chocolate Sauce;
    Hot Fudge Sauce
Chocolate Terrine with
    Chocolate and Strawberry
    Drizzles, 86–87
Chocolate Truffle-Vanilla Bean
    Ice Cream, 156–57

Chocolate Wafer Crust, 74
Chocolate Walnut Tart, 114–16
Chocolate Zucchini Cake, 28–29
Chopping chocolate, 7
Classic Fudge, 44–45
Classification of chocolate, 2–5
Cocoa. *See also* Hot Chocolate
  Angel Food Cake, 142–43
    with Strawberry Whip,
    26–27
  butter, 1–5
  Frosting, Easy, 20–21
  powder, 2, 4
Coconut-Pecan Frosting, 18–19
Coeur à la Creme, White
    Chocolate, 104–5
Coffee Crunch, Blum's, 145
Compound coatings, 4
Conching (of cacao beans), 1
Cookies. *See also* Bar Cookies;
    Brownies
  Cakey Chocolate Chip-Raisin,
    60–61
  Chewy Chocolate and White
    Chocolate Chip, 62–63
  Chocolate-Dipped Orange,
    106–7
  Texas Pecan and Chocolate
    Toffee, 58–59
Couverture chocolate, 2–3
Cranberry Chocolate
    Cheesecake, 74–75
Cream, whipped, 11. *See also*
    Ganache; Strawberry Whip
Cream Pie, Parker House,
    150–51
Creaming (butter), 9
Curls, chocolate, 13

Dacquoise. *See* Marjolaine
    Classique
Dad's Famous Rocky Road,
    50–51
Decorations, chocolate, 13–14
Devil's Food Cake with Fudgy
    Frosting, 32–33

Diane's Triple-Layered Delights, 64–65
Double boiler method of melting chocolate, 8
Double Chocolate–Sour Cream Layer Cake, 16–17
Dream Bars, Impossible, 66
Droste Cocoa powder (alkalized), 4
Dutch-process (alkalized) cocoa powder, 4

Easy Cocoa Frosting, 20–21
Eggs and egg whites, 9
Espresso Syrup, 108–9

Flour, about, 10
Food and Drug Administration standards for chocolate, 2
Fondue, Tropical Chocolate, with Seasonal Fruits, 102
Frosting. See also Icing; Glazes; Strawberry Whip
  Buttercream, 122–24
  Chocolate–Sour Cream, 16–17
  Coconut-Pecan, 18–19
  Easy Cocoa, 20–21
  Fudgy, 32–33
  White Marshmallow, 24–25
Fudge
  Classic, 44–45
  Flavored, 45
  Make-it-Easy, 42–43
  Nut, 45
Fudge Ripple Ice Cream, Strawberry, 146–47
Fudge Sauce, Schrafft's Famous Hot, 153
Fudge Tart, Raspberry-Topped, 130–31
Fudge Torte, San Andreas, 132–33
Fudgy Frosting, 32–33

Galax leaves (chocolate), 14
Ganache, 92–94, 95–96, 98–99
Garnishes, 13–14

Genoise, 92–94, 122–23
German Chocolate Cake with Coconut-Pecan Frosting, 18–19
Glaze(s). See also Icing
  bittersweet chocolate, 74–75, 78–79
  semisweet chocolate, 36–37
  shiny cocoa, 95–96
Gold Rush Sundae, 139
Golden Gate Ice Cream Pie, 144
Grand Indulgence Hot Chocolate, 101
Grand Marnier Truffles, 88–89
Great American Chocolate Festival, 101

Hazelnuts, toasting and skinning, 10
Heavy whipping cream, 11
Hershey's Cocoa powder (nonalkalized), 4
Homemade Chocolate Syrup, 138
Hot Chocolate, Grand Indulgence, 101
Hot Fudge Sauce, Schrafft's Famous, 153

Ice Cream
  Chocolate Peppermint Chip, 154–55
  Chocolate Truffle–Vanilla Bean, 156–57
  Strawberry Fudge Ripple, 146–47
  Sundae, Gold Rush, 139
Ice Cream Pie, Golden Gate, 144
Ice Cream Soda, Black and White, 148
Icing. See also Frosting; Glaze(s)
  cocoa buttermilk, 30–31
  for Parker House Cream Pie, 150–51
Instant dissolving sugar, 11
Ivy leaves (chocolate), 14

Irish Cream–Chip Cheesecake, 134–35

Kiss Kookies, 56–57

Layer Cake. See Cake
Leaves, chocolate, 14
Lemon leaves (chocolate), 14
Lemon Tart, Bittersweet, 112–13
Lindt Blancor. See White chocolate
Liquor, chocolate, 1–2
Loaf Cake. See also Pound Cake; Tea Bread
  Banana-Chocolate, 38–39
Lois's Brownies, 54–55

Macadamia nuts, 10
Macadamia Milk Chocolate Crunch, 46–47
Make-it-Easy Chocolate Fudge, 42–43
Malteds, Chocolate, in Chocolate Bags, 140–41
Margarine, 9
Marjolaine Classique, 81–83
Marquise au chocolat. See Chocolate Terrine with Chocolate and Strawberry Drizzles
Marshmallow
  -based fudge, 42–43
  frosting, 24–25
  -studded brownies, 54–55
Mascarpone, 108–9
Mayonnaise Cake, Chocolate, 20–21
Measuring ingredients, 10–11
Meltaways, Chocolate–Peanut Butter, 48–49
Melting chocolate, 7–9
Meringues. See Marjolaine Classique
Microwave oven
  for making chocolate curls, 13
  for melting chocolate, 8
  for softening butter, 9

Milk chocolate, 3
  and Peanut Butter Brownies,
    51
  Macadamia Crunch, 46–47
Mississippi Mud Cake, 70–71
Mix-in-the-pan cake. *See* Wicky
    Wacky Chocolate Cake
Mousse
  Passion Fruit, 125–27
  Pie, Chocolate Orange, 120–21
  Spuma de Caffé Latte, 110–11
My Dad's Famous Rocky Road,
    50–51

Nonalkalized (natural) cocoa
    powder, 4
North Beach Chocolate Sauce,
    152
Nuts, about, 11

One-bowl cake. *See* Wicky
    Wacky Chocolate Cake
Orange
  -Chocolate Bundt Cake, 36–37
  Chocolate Mousse Pie, 120–21
  Cookies, Chocolate-Dipped,
    106–7
  liqueur. *See* Grand Marnier
Original German Chocolate
    Cake with Coconut-Pecan
    Frosting, 18–19

Parker House Cream Pie, 150–51
Passion fruit
  and White Chocolate Tart,
    125–27
  and White Chocolate Truffles,
    90–91
Passionate White Chocolate
    Truffles, 90–91
Peanut(s)
  Pie, Chocolate, 68–69
  unsalted, 10
Peanut Butter
  Blossoms. *See* Kiss Kookies

–Chocolate Meltaways, 48–49
and Milk Chocolate Brownies,
    50–51
Pecan(s)
  and Chocolate Toffee Cookies,
    58–59
  -Coconut Frosting, 18–19
  Diane's Triple-Layered
    Delights, 64–65
  toasting, 10
Peppermint
  Black and White Cake, 25
  Chocolate Chip Ice Cream,
    154–55
Pie. *See also* Cheesecake
  Chocolate Orange Mousse,
    120–21
  Chocolate Peanut, 68–69
  Ice Cream, Golden Gate, 144
  Parker House Cream, 150–51
Pineapple-Rum Truffles, 91
Pistachio-White Chocolate Tea
    Bread, 117–19
Pound Cake
  Berry and Chocolate
    Sandwich, 128–29
  White Chocolate-Pistachio Tea
    Bread, 117–19
  Chocolate, 22–23
Premelted chocolate, 4
Pudding
  Bread, Chocolate-Raisin, 67
  Chocolate Banana Cream, 149

Raisin-Chocolate Bread
    Pudding, 67
Raisin-Chocolate Chip Cookies,
    Cakey, 60–61
Raspberry(ies)
  Berry and Chocolate
    Sandwich, 128–29
  Chocolate Trifle, 84–85
  Sauce for White Chocolate
    Coeur à la Creme, 104–5
  -Topped Fudge Tart, 130–31

Rigo Jansci, 95–97
Rocky Road, My Dad's Famous,
    50–51
Rose(s)
  glazed, 122
  syrup, 122

Sachertorte, 78–79
Salted butter, about, 9
San Andreas Fudge Torte,
    132–33
Sauce
  North Beach Chocolate, 152
  Raspberry, 104–5
  Schrafft's Famous Hot Fudge,
    153
  Strawberry Drizzle, 86–87
Schrafft's Famous Hot Fudge
    Sauce, 153
"Seizing" (of chocolate), 7–8
Semisweet chocolate, 3–4
  glaze, 36–37
Soda, Ice Cream, Black and
    White, 148
Sour Cream–Double Chocolate
    Layer Cake, 16–17
Spuma de Caffé Latte, 110–11
Storing chocolate, 8
Strawberry(ies)
  Berry and Chocolate
    Sandwich, 128–29
  Drizzle Sauce, 86–87
  Fudge Ripple Ice Cream,
    146–47
  Whip, 26–27
Sugar, about, 11
Sugar syrup, 92–93
Summer coatings, 4
Sundae, Gold Rush, 139
Superfine sugar, 11
Sweet (unsalted) butter, about, 9
Sweet chocolate, about, 3
Swiss Truffle Loaf, 92–94
Syrup
  Chocolate, 86–87, 138